Staying the Course

Staying the Course

A Guide of Best Practices for School Leaders

Sheila E. Sapp

ROWMAN & LITTLEFIELD
Lanham • Boulder • New York • London

Published by Rowman & Littlefield
An imprint of The Rowman & Littlefield Publishing Group, Inc.
4501 Forbes Boulevard, Suite 200, Lanham, Maryland 20706
www.rowman.com

Unit A, Whitacre Mews, 26-34 Stannary Street, London SE11 4AB

Copyright © 2019 by Sheila E. Sapp

All rights reserved. No part of this book may be reproduced in any form or by any electronic or mechanical means, including information storage and retrieval systems, without written permission from the publisher, except by a reviewer who may quote passages in a review.

British Library Cataloguing in Publication Information Available

Library of Congress Cataloging-in-Publication Data Available

ISBN 9781475845655 (electronic) | ISBN 9781475845624 (cloth : alk. paper) | ISBN 9781475845648 (pbk. : alk. paper)

∞ ™ The paper used in this publication meets the minimum requirements of American National Standard for Information Sciences Permanence of Paper for Printed Library Materials, ANSI/NISO Z39.48-1992.

Printed in the United States of America

To my mother, Eva E. Henry,
who provided support and encouragement throughout my life.
Also, I am grateful to Dr. Noel Carroll
for his foresight, leadership, and confidence in my ability to lead a school.

Contents

Foreword		ix
Preface		xi
Acknowledgments		xiii
Introduction		xv
1	Tried-and-True Principles: Building Blocks for Developing Resiliency	1
2	The Good, Bad, and Ugly: Learning Lessons from Successes, Messes, and Mistakes	15
3	Time and Energy Stealers: Maintaining High-Maintenance Problem Personnel	53
4	School Leaders Need Love Too: Coping with Criticism, Stress, and Anxiety	71
5	If Only You Could Do It Over Again: Looking Back and Moving Forward	87
Conclusion		105
Bibliography		107
About the Author		109

Foreword

I have known Dr. Sheila Sapp for over two decades. During the time we worked together, Dr. Sapp guided educators through her work as a principal and curriculum director. She was a hands-on administrator, always looking for creative and impactful ways to approach the difficult obstacles often embedded in educational scenarios.

Principals face many challenges and mandates to which the public is oblivious. They face stressful situations daily that can cause the most dedicated person to bend and sometimes break. In her book, Dr. Sapp strives to offer proven methods to help school administrators *stay the course*.

This book is a gold mine of ideas and inspirations for beginning and seasoned school administrators. In her retirement, Dr. Sapp continues to share with and care about those who are shaping the future of our young generation of students. This, her latest book, is a must for a principal's library.

Dr. Ann Proctor
Retired Superintendent of Camden County Schools
Kingsland, Georgia

Preface

Effective schools research studies have highlighted the importance of school administrators being instructional leaders and change agents in their buildings. Focus on academic achievement and improving instructional effectiveness are two critical aspects of a school leader's instructional leadership role. In addition to improving classroom instructional practices and implementing curricular changes, school leaders have the responsibility of supervising staff and managing overall school operations. Meanwhile, they are expected to handle changes without losing their focus. With this type of pressure in a challenging environment, the question is: How are school leaders able to stay the course and maintain their effectiveness?

It is evident that school administrators need to have up-to-date skills, knowledge, and best practices to operate effective and efficient schools. The author of this book seeks to expand the knowledge base and best practices by further examining strategies, recommendations, and tools used by current and former school administrators. To guarantee a continuous legacy of effective leaders to successfully meet the ever-changing needs of schools, we need to continue to explore what strategies, principles, qualities, techniques, and best practices enable school administrators to lead schools to levels of higher academic achievement and staff performance.

This book also addresses and shares constructive ways for school leaders to cope with criticism, stress, anxiety, and problem personnel without compromising their decisions, beliefs, and values. There are real-life scenarios presented that school administrators faced with plausible solutions and recommendations for consideration and possible implementation. The scenarios portrayed offer readers an inside view of other school leaders' decision-making processes, resolutions, and strategies.

Managing and supervising staff is another aspect of instructional leadership that is time consuming and emotionally draining for school leaders of today. School leaders must have the ability to work with a variety of personalities and skill levels in their buildings. They are faced with the challenge of providing the assistance and resources needed to help staff grow professionally without becoming weighted down with *problem staff* baggage. The author discusses selected high-maintenance personnel or time stealers that negatively impact the school and staff. Strategies are proposed by the author to assist school leaders in thwarting the negative effects of high-maintenance personnel on themselves and staff.

Additionally, federal/state mandates, public cries for accountability, and disgruntled teachers' comments heighten an already-challenging environment for school leaders. Once school leaders become stressed and anxious about their performance and decisions, they begin to doubt their leadership ability, knowledge, and skills. School leaders who are fearful, stressed, and over anxious are unable to maintain their focus on school goals or initiatives. Also, obtaining buy-in and support from school clientele becomes an uphill battle, thereby compounding stress and anxiety. Readers are advised to protect and rejuvenate themselves through recommended tips and on-the-job strategies to relieve tension and stress.

Acknowledgments

I am grateful to the students, teachers, and parents who helped me grow personally and professionally during my career. Special gratitude is extended to Dr. Darlene Bruce and Dr. Deborah Milstead, who provided insights and support for this venture. Additionally, I am eternally appreciative of my daughter, Dr. Nicholyn Hutchinson, an editor, critic, and sounding board for my endeavors. Finally, I am forever grateful for the continued support, assistance, and never-ending blessings of my husband, Everette.

Introduction

Successful leaders see opportunities in every difficulty rather than the difficulty in every opportunity.—Reed Markham

You have pursued and successfully obtained one of the most respected positions in a school system—a principalship. As it turns out, it is also one of the most demanding.

Now, not only are you responsible for ensuring students receive a quality education and excellent teachers, but you are also required by the superintendent to move the school forward. Already this is strenuous work, but it will continue to get harder as goal posts move.

School administrators face federal/state mandates and system-driven objectives while tackling everyday issues in their jobs as they arise. They must balance improving schools and increasing test scores under the critical glare of public scrutiny. For school leaders, there is no hiding from judgment and escaping accountability.

You became a principal because you are passionate about education and want to make an impact in your role, but how do you persevere and remain focused when times get tough? When there is a tricky issue to address, what is the best step to take to resolve this sensitive problem? When you have had a frustrating and draining day, how do you remain positive and not dread returning to your building in the morning?

Written by a former principal with more than forty years of experience, *Staying the Course* is a practical guide that answers these and other questions and helps principals navigate some of the difficult terrain they will cross along their school leadership journey.

School instructional leadership has increasingly become a high-risk role and detrimentally impacts the emotional and mental health of school administrators. With the continuing rise of expectations, school leaders must have basic principles and qualities as foundational guideposts for their decisions and actions. Chapter 1 focuses on selected principles and qualities to empower leaders and foster meaningful relationships. Also, readers are shown the importance of possessing emotional resilience to strengthen the ability to adapt when confronted with challenges, issues, and unexpected changes.

Another aspect of your role that monopolizes the day is addressing student discipline and dealing with personnel issues. You spend countless hours resolving incidents, interviewing witnesses, and determining consequences for infractions. Wouldn't it be helpful to explore other administrators' methods for handling student, parent, and teacher concerns? In chapter 2, you are exposed to a variety of real-life incidents administrators experienced and resolved effectively. Additionally, you'll attain a plethora of rationales, resolutions, and strategies to review for possible implementation.

Supervising and monitoring staff encompasses a substantial portion of every administrator's day. Therefore, you must manage your time judiciously to address individual staff development and professional growth needs. Occasionally, there are staff members who consume time and energy unnecessarily, thus minimizing your effectiveness. Chapter 3 describes and suggests truths, strategies, and recommendations to counteract the effect of time stealers on school staff and morale.

Today's challenging school environments pose a threat to every school leader's effectiveness and well-being. Principals are easy targets for public critics, unhappy parents, and dissatisfied staff by virtue of their position. Being a recipient of constant criticism and negative comments weakens self-confidence and the ability to weather storms. Doubting your capabilities or decisions opens the door to stress. To avoid stress and a descent into ineptness or mediocracy, learn viable ways to protect, support, and rejuvenate yourself. In chapter 4, you'll learn how to accept criticism and negative comments in an appropriate manner. Also featured in this chapter are aids for handling stress and anxiety. Additionally, listings of recommended techniques and supplemental resources are included for review and possible implementation.

Most of your time is focused on increasing academic achievement and improving schools. How are you updating your skills to meet future changes and challenges? Do you know your strengths and areas needing growth? How are you determining the effectiveness of decisions made and actions taken? Or, are you doing things the way you have always done them? If it's important for teachers to update their skills and knowledge for relevancy, how are you promoting and encouraging *your* professional growth and personal development?

Reflection and self-reflection are two tools presented in chapter 5 that allow and foster continuous professional and personal growth. The author offers reflection and self-reflection as workable tools to implement during the workday to assess a leader's effectiveness and efficiency. You'll also have the opportunity to learn about the benefits of reflection and self-reflection along with suggested applications to consider for possible implementation. As an added feature, the author includes self-reflection questions and responses of current and former retired administrators for additional insights and perspectives.

This book is organized to allow individuals to read chapters based on specific interests and needs. Each chapter concludes with a summary and a "Going Deeper" section to extend thinking and encourage the application of ideas and activities provided. The author's overall goal is to inspire current and aspiring school administrators to lead courageously and *stay the course*.

Chapter One

Tried-and-True Principles

Building Blocks for Developing Resiliency

School leaders face the challenge of continuously improving schools and guaranteeing academic growth for all students. Effective leaders know how to manage schools, serve as instructional leaders, and implement viable changes. We know the significant role school administrators play in improving teachers' classroom instructional performance and utilization of effective instructional practices. School leaders are charged with responding to cries for accountability and increased test scores. How do school leaders remain positive and maintain their focus without becoming frustrated by new mandates, budget cuts, and unexpected changes?

This chapter briefly explores how school leaders develop resiliency to help them maintain their effectiveness as they endure changes and challenges. In addition to examining their resiliency, presented are selected principles and qualities school leaders perceived as necessary to help them stay focused on school goals and initiatives. These recommended selected principles, qualities, and strategies serve as foundational building blocks to developing resiliency for school administrators. Resiliency enables and equips principals with the ability to withstand changes and adapt to shifting public and school system demands throughout their careers.

RESILIENCY FOR SCHOOL LEADERS

We know the vital role school leaders play as instructional leaders and change agents in their schools. Research studies have espoused the relationship between a school leader's effectiveness as an instructional leader and student achievement. The effective schools studies examined what school leaders did to foster and promote academic growth and success for all students in their schools. Emphasis was placed on tasks leaders performed such as monitoring classroom instruction and supervising teachers. These tasks related to instructional leadership are centered on specific tasks or duties school administrators perform.

The ever-increasing public scrutiny of schools, cries for accountability, and the rapid pace of change require school leaders to be skillful as well as emotionally strong. Emotional strength, resiliency, is needed to bounce back from disappointments, obstacles, and frustrations. Like many service-oriented professions, school leaders spend most of their time addressing needs and giving themselves to students, teachers, and parents. In many instances, this attention and focus on their school clientele is not reciprocated. School administrators are in danger of feeling unappreciated, weary, and worn emotionally if they rely solely on their staff for sustenance.

School leaders must be emotionally resilient, be principled, and possess selective qualities to manage and operate effective schools. As the instructional leader in a building, administrators must have the ability to work with people to foster and encourage continuous growth and professional development. School- and system-level goals for school improvement and high academic achievement for all students are unattainable if a school is not led appropriately. Operating and developing an effective and efficient school requires an understanding of how to respond to people and meet their needs.

Administrators sometimes struggle with handling and understanding their own needs. Many universities and colleges do not offer comprehensive training on coping with human emotional needs for current and aspiring school leaders. Most of what is learned about meeting the needs of school clientele is acquired on the job through years of experience and lessons learned. It is critical for school leaders to learn how to care for themselves and remain emotionally strong as they encounter frustrations and disappointments, address needs, and face issues throughout their day.

Also, school administrators must accept giving of themselves without receiving anything in return. Feelings of having nothing else to give among school leaders lead to burn out and self-doubt. Remaining emotionally resilient helps principals weather whatever storms or changes that may arise. An emotionally resilient school leader has a keen sense of his or her capabilities, strengths, and weaknesses. He or she manages feelings, renews self, and sustains an emotional balance. When changes occur, emotionally resilient administrators understand their clientele's needs as well as their own. They'll continue to move schools positively forward.

Developing Emotional Resiliency

How do school leaders really cope with frustrations, changes, and demands they encounter? For some administrators, masking their true feelings is how they get through the day. They may use the following coping strategies to protect themselves emotionally. They take risks, behave out of character, avoid challenges, mask their true selves, stay in their comfort zone, and disconnect from their feelings or emotions. School leaders using these coping strategies may be perceived as uncaring, insincere, weak, unsupportive, and lacking enthusiasm or passion for their job.

School leaders develop and strengthen their emotional resilience by knowing and understanding themselves better. They take time to examine their beliefs and values. School leaders who are rooted in their values don't change their behavior or disrupt their moral compass. They know and understand who they are; they are not afraid to show their emotions. Emotional resilience is nurtured through encouraging others and building relationships with staff.

Their goal is to foster and encourage emotional bonds among their staff, which are needed to manage and lead a school. They focus on strategies that empower and build self-esteem.

Building Emotional Resiliency

School administrators are humans and have feelings too. They need space to step away from the shield of *principalship* and check their emotional state. It is not enough to just get through the day and mask concerns about the school and solutions for issues. Principals need to get the support necessary to help them bounce back from situations or incidents that are draining. Seeking support to maintain emotional resilience is not a sign of weakness. Leaders who seek support and assistance if needed can:

- develop their authenticity as a leader;
- build and develop a better understanding of their emotional resilience;
- be viewed as compassionate and caring; and
- be their true selves.

How Do You Begin?

The steps to follow for developing emotional resilience are simple and easy to implement. School leaders start with the desire to know themselves better as people first. Understand who you are and know the values that drive your behavior, actions, and decisions.

See leadership as a process of building and developing meaningful relationships with the people you lead. Believe in everyone's self-worth and importance to the organization. Share your leadership among your staff, and allow them to lead while you guide.

Be willing to ask yourself the following questions:

- What kind of life am I living now as the school leader?
- What kind of life do I want to live as the school leader?
- How do I get to where I want to be if I am not there?
- Are my emotional needs being met as the school leader?

Responses to these questions pave the way to examining leadership styles and current levels of emotional resiliency. Administrators who find themselves lacking in either of these areas can seek professional learning to improve their emotional resilience and leadership style.

Tried-and-True Principles

School leaders who have spent extended tenure as successful elementary principals attribute their sustainability and longevity to selected principles they deem necessary for effective leadership. They have been able to weather changes, challenges, and mandates without losing their sense of direction or focus throughout their careers. They see their role as an important integral component for school improvement, but they also recognize the importance of principles or qualities leaders need to possess to enable them to stay the course as they strive to attain school goals and system initiatives.

Following is a list of principles and strategies recommended to serve as qualities needed by school leaders to assist them in running effective and efficient schools. These selected principles are not all inclusive but serve as additional resources and guideposts for current and aspiring school administrators. The recommended strategies provide a repertoire of techniques for school administrators to consider for review or implementation.

Patience

> *Let me tell you the secret that has led to my goal. My strength lies in my tenacity.*—Louis Pasteur

As a school leader, patience is a principle that is hard to keep in the forefront. Most school administrators, as change agents and instructional leaders, want to see changes and growth right away. Everyone wants higher test scores and school goals met overnight. School leaders desire to have their efforts and challenging work come to fruition as soon as possible. Change is a process. Any change involving teachers, students, parents, programs, and school initiatives will manifest in the future. You can't have a definite time frame for things that have many factors or variables that are not within a school leader's sphere of control.

Strategies for Patience
- Set realistic timelines for School Improvement Plans or initiatives.
- Map out key status checkpoints or progress evaluations.
- Celebrate small steps or milestones accomplished along the way.
- Monitor progress and effectiveness of interventions and/or assessments.
- Update School Improvement Plans or initiatives as changes are made.
- Inform staff and public about progress, changes, growth, and setbacks.
- Think positively about challenges.

Perseverance

> *Great works are performed not by strength but by perseverance.* —Samuel Johnson

It is easy to hang in there and keep plugging away when things are going smoothly. School leaders face many unexpected challenges, situations, and experiences when operating and managing a school. There may be a personnel issue or behavior situation that consumes a major part of the instructional day. Or a principal may be struggling trying to fill a key teacher slot with no apparent applicants in sight. The easiest thing to do is to give in to these unforeseen challenges and worry. Uncertainty can lead to anxiety. Perseverance, however, leads to strength.

Strategies for Perseverance
- Seek outside resources for additional assistance.
- Think outside the box.
- Stay focused on your goal or objectives.
- Explore and implement anxiety-releasing interventions.
- Dispel negative thoughts.
- Renew yourself physically and emotionally, if needed.

Empathy

> *Leadership is about empathy. It is about having the ability to relate to and connect with people for the purpose of inspiring and empowering their lives.*
> —Oprah Winfrey

Being able to walk in someone else's shoes is paramount to a school leader's role in a school. Whether or not a school is managed and operated effectively depends on how well a leader builds and develops relationships with his or her school clientele. School administrators who are excellent human relationship builders enlist their staff's support and accomplish long- and short-term school goals. Their teachers feel supported and are empowered to become leaders themselves. They know their administrators care about them as classroom teachers and people. Teachers who feel appreciated, understood, and cared for become caring teachers for students.

Strategies for Empathy
- Seek to understand feelings and emotions.
- Communicate with school clientele.
- Learn personal and professional things about staff, students, and parents.
- Address personal and professional needs of school clientele, if needed.
- Celebrate and recognize personal and professional accomplishments.
- View situations, incidents, and classrooms through the lenses of school clientele.
- Show you care.
- Be human and open to other points of view, opinions, and ideas.

Sympathy

> *The purpose of human life is to serve, and to show compassion and the will to help others.*—Albert Schweitzer

Many school leaders, like other service-oriented careers, don't have difficulty displaying sympathy or exhibiting compassion for clientele they serve. As a matter of fact, most people enter the field of education to help and serve others. School administrators need to exercise caution when using sympathy. Being too sympathetic and compassionate can thwart intellectual growth and professional development. If this occurs, objectivity is lost, and school leaders are unable to help individuals in their buildings. Teachers who are overly sympathetic with students limit or lower their expectations and requirements.

Strategies for Sympathy
- Address specific needs only.
- Acknowledge their pain or feelings.
- Serve as a mentor and resource.
- Show your concern and remain objective.
- Avoid their total dependency on you.
- Offer help in a concrete way.

Connect

> *Children may forget what you say, but they'll never forget how you make them feel.*—Parker J. Palmer

How do you connect with individuals and stakeholders in your building? Do you go out of your way to communicate and establish relationships? Do you interact with students daily? Or do you simply rely on your position or role to establish relationships? Remember, everyone on some level wants to be recognized and valued. How do you gain information about your staff and students to connect? Do you keep a notebook or review staff and student information sheets? Below are examples of ways to connect effectively throughout the school year.

Strategies to Connect
- Greet whoever you meet daily with a genuine smile.
- Visit classrooms and ask students questions about what they're learning.
- Inquire about a new baby brother or sister, new shoes, a missing tooth, and a haircut.
- Be where students, staff, parents, and other stakeholders are. Initiate quality conversations.
- Share information about yourself with staff, students, and stakeholders.
- Spend time in the cafeteria, at the bus port, on the playground, and walking the halls.
- Attend games, performances, and recitals of your staff's children and students.
- Be present physically, mentally, emotionally, and socially every day.
- Celebrate birthdays with special *Happy Birthday* pencils and note cards.

Be Authentic

> *Let the world know who you are, not as you think you should be, because sooner or later, if you are posing, you will forget the pose, and then where are you?*—Fanny Brice

Many school leaders have a mentor or role model they admire or wish to emulate. Principals are walking billboards and must always be conscious of the messages projected to teachers, students, parents, and other stakeholders. It is easy to admire a colleague or peer and attempt to be like them. It is very important for leaders to develop a style of leadership that reflects their authentic self. If you portray someone else, your duplicity will be unveiled quickly. It doesn't take long to uncover insincerity and hypocrisy. The quote from Hamlet "To thine own self be true" is good advice for all school leaders. Make sure all actions and behaviors represent the authentic you.

Strategies for Being Authentic
- Walk the walk and talk the talk.
- Stand behind what you say and do.

- Base decisions and actions on personal beliefs and values.
- Select a mentor or role model whose beliefs and values align with yours.
- Be genuine and sincere.

Be Honest

> *Honest hearts produce honest actions.* —Brigham Young

Honesty is an age-old principle that will never become passé. As a matter of fact, the world would be a better place if more people were honest. Imagine intentionally dispensing false information to a student, teacher, or parent. Being honest is the hallmark of being a person of character. Trust can't be cultivated among stakeholders if the school leader is viewed as not trustworthy. There will be times due to the sensitivity of the situation that school administrators are not authorized to divulge certain facts or have discussions. However, incidents of this nature should be handled in such a manner as to keep their honesty and integrity intact.

Strategies for Being Honest
- Stick to the facts.
- If you are not authorized to disclose certain information, say so.
- Confirm information received before sharing with stakeholders.
- Make decisions based on accurate information received.
- Don't say or do anything you can't support or defend.

Be a Listener

> *Most people do not listen with the intent to understand; they listen with the intent to reply.* —Stephen Covey

Listening. It seems like a simple task, yet very few people are good listeners. While listening to someone, are you waiting for the opportunity to interrupt? Or do you promptly provide an answer that doesn't address what was really needed? Being an effective listener is critical for school leaders who spend a major portion of their day listening. They need to ensure responses are appropriate answers to questions, concerns, issues, and requests from clientele. Every administrator should become skilled listeners and make a concerted effort to improve.

Strategies for Being a Listener
- Refrain from interrupting, and listen.
- Wait for individuals to finish their statement(s) before responding.
- Take brief notes on key points for documentation.

- Summarize and restate what was said as a check for understanding.
- Ask for clarifications, if needed.
- Practice silence.
- Remove or avoid distractions.
- Watch for nonverbal communication and tone of voice.
- Think before responding.
- Empathize, sympathize, and show an interest.

Be Forgiving

> *The weak can never forgive. Forgiveness is an attribute of the strong.* —Mahatma Gandhi

There are no perfect teachers, students, parents, or school administrators. Everyone makes a mistake or has a difficult day. School leaders should not walk around wearing feelings on their sleeves. When working with people, you are bound to become a target for misplaced anger or blame. Administrators are expected to do what is right and not seek revenge if mistreated by staff. Accusations and name-calling can pierce armors occasionally. Remember not to take venting by upset stakeholders or frustrated teachers personally. Forgiving is not compromising or giving in to someone. Forgiving others enables you to be forgiven also.

Strategies for Being Forgiving
- Develop a thick skin.
- Put yourself in the other person's shoes.
- Remain calm and professional.
- Be nonjudgmental.
- Learn to let go.
- Forgive others and yourself.
- Seek peace.

Be Kind

> *Kindness is a language which the deaf can hear, and the blind can see.* —Mark Twain

We live in a world of technology in which iPhones, iPads, laptops, and desktops surround us. The human touch and displays of kindness are almost becoming endangered. As a matter of fact, any kind gesture or act of generosity is a noteworthy event. Students and families are starving for attention, affection, and self-worth. It is amazing how uplifting and powerful a smile or kind gesture is for a troubled student, a parent, or a newly hired staff member. Kindness gives high dividends for investments and has unlimited benefits.

Strategies for Being Kind
- Surprise your office staff with a box of donuts.
- Greet everyone with a genuine smile daily.
- Call or send cards to unwell employees and students.
- Read to a class or offer to teach a subject to relieve a teacher.
- Sing or say "Happy Birthday" to staff, students, and stakeholders.
- Tie shoestrings and locate lost backpacks.
- Care for others genuinely.
- Be kind to yourself.
- Smile.
- Offer water, tea, or coffee to staff, parents, and visitors.
- Hold doors, and provide chairs for senior citizens.

Be a Delegator

> *If you want to do a few small things right, do them yourself. If you want to do great things and make a big impact, learn to delegate.* —John C. Maxwell

Delegating is a skill that is a source of difficulty for many principals. Some school leaders fear losing control and their authority. Others suffer from a *me* rather than *we* complex and believe if you want something done right, do it yourself. Those who do delegate responsibilities or tasks often micromanage staff during the entire process, fearing dropped balls or missed deadlines. Relinquishing control and delegating projects to capable staff enhances a school leader's ability to grow and develop future leaders. Leaders are not expected to be strong in all areas. Delegating allows administrators to tap into and use existing talents and skills.

Strategies for Being a Delegator
- Assess the abilities and skills of your staff.
- Delegate to the right people.
- Decide which tasks to delegate.
- Create a climate and culture that stimulates and encourages creativity.
- Be open to and accepting of ideas and different perspectives.
- Be clear on directions, deadlines, and expectations.
- Monitor the progress of the task without micromanaging.
- Utilize the strengths and skills of others to accomplish school goals or initiatives.
- Empower others by assigning them projects or tasks to lead or supervise.
- Recognize and trust the ability of others to perform successfully.

Be Humorous

> *Like a welcome summer rain, humor may suddenly cleanse and cool the earth, the air, and you.* —Langston Hughes

It is hard to find the humor or even want to laugh after experiencing a trying situation. Nor is it easy to laugh when you are the brunt of a joke. Laughter is a way to loosen tight muscles and clenched teeth while remaining professional through a verbal attack of a dissatisfied parent or hurt staff member. Being able to take a deep breath and see the humor in tough situations is a tool that benefits everyone. Laughter and humor ease tense situations and relieve stress. Humor helps school leaders look at the lighter side of things and recover quicker from situations that may dampen spirits.

Strategies for Being Humorous
- Develop a sense of humor by finding out what makes you laugh.
- Look for the lighter side of situations and events.
- Try not to take everything and yourself too seriously.
- Laugh at yourself from time to time.
- Find the humor in positive and negative things.
- Step back and laugh when you find yourself in a tense situation.

Be Sincere

> *Sincerity is impossible unless it pervades the whole being, and the pretense of it saps the very foundation of character.* —James Russell Lowell

It is said you can fool some people some of the time, but you can't fool all people all the time. It doesn't take children or adults a long time to figure out there is something wrong in Denmark. Administrators are the center of attention in every school. Actions and decisions are scrutinized by staff, parents, and stakeholders. Once you are found to have a character flaw of insincerity, your effectiveness as a school leader is damaged beyond repair. Efforts to regain credibility are an uphill battle on a slippery slope. Sincerity as a principle or character trait is more vital for a leader than leadership skills. No one follows the lead of a disingenuous person or administrator.

Strategies for Being Sincere
- Be true to your values and beliefs.
- Stand before and behind what you say or do.
- Let your actions reflect who you are.
- Treat people with respect.
- Show and be the real you in all situations.

- Be genuine.
- Do good without reward.
- Use positive affirmations.
- Say only the truth.

Be Resilient

> *Do not judge me by my success, judge me by how many times I fell down and got back up again.*—Nelson Mandela

The work life of school administrators is beset with challenges and sometimes overwhelming situations. School leaders face pressures to increase academic achievement and guarantee success for all. In addition to developing strategies and intervention plans to ensure growth for students, school administrators address and resolve other issues or concerns that may arise in their buildings on any given day. What do administrators do when their interventions or strategies yield few results? How do they bounce back from disappointing test scores or an unexpected loss or transfer of a highly effective staff member?

Principals keep strategizing, brainstorming, planning, goal setting, and problem solving. Each setback is met with a *we can get through this* attitude. It is this spirit that enables principals to turn corners and focus on goals no matter what roadblocks or changes are encountered. Resilient administrators see beyond momentary roadblocks and press onward.

Strategies for Being Resilient
- Stay focused on goals and targets.
- Be open to suggestions and out-of-the-box thinking.
- Be willing to continually reassess and reevaluate to improve effectiveness.
- Be positive and forward thinking.
- See failures as growth opportunities.
- Find a sense of purpose for your life.
- Embrace change.
- Develop problem-solving skills.
- Build positive beliefs in your abilities.
- Keep growing and learning.
- Celebrate the small wins.
- Stay tough and pick yourself up.

CHAPTER 1 SUMMARY

Despite the ever-changing landscape of school reform, increasing quests for excellence, and continuing cries for academic achievement, schools and students are succeeding. Chapter 1 presented ten selected principles school leaders possessed enabling them to lead effectively. Additionally, this chapter provided recommended strategies to develop the selected principles to enhance leaders' effectiveness and success. These selected principles and strategies shared are not all-inclusive. There are other principles and strategies that lend themselves to building and establishing strong foundations for the principalship.

GOING DEEPER

Time to Reflect

1. Which principle(s) or quality(ies) do you currently possess?
2. Are there any principles you would like to acquire based on your current or past experiences?
3. On a scale from 1 to 10, with 1 being the highest, rate yourself on the principles presented in chapter 1.
4. Is there a principle you would like to develop or strengthen?
5. Write a professional learning plan for the principle(s) you want to acquire.
6. Of the selected principles presented in chapter 1, which principle, in your opinion, is the most critical for administrators?
7. Select a mentor or close associate to serve as your accountability partner to assess and monitor your progress.
8. What resources will you use to strengthen or acquire desired principles?

Chapter Two

The Good, Bad, and Ugly

Learning Lessons from Successes, Messes, and Mistakes

> *Experience is not what happens to a man. It is what a man does with what happens to him.* —Aldous Leonard Huxley

We have all heard the saying "If life hands you lemons, make lemonade." School leaders daily face situations that are *lemons*. Handling *lemons* provides school administrators with valuable lessons and sometimes unique resolutions. These experiences and lessons are not found in college textbooks or online. Administrators gain and expand their "How to" or "What to Do" tool kits for real-life incidents, successes, mistakes, and messes from all situations that occur. These true-to-life scenarios will provide different perspectives and additional strategies for handling similar incidents or situations in their building.

LATE-AFTERNOON PHONE CALLS

All school leaders strive to be accessible and available whenever needed by staff and stakeholders. Many have an *open-door* policy encouraging people to drop in any time. This policy sometimes is extended to receiving and answering telephone calls. Have you ever been heading out of your office at the end of a tiring day and the phone rings? You stop, answer the phone, and spend the next thirty to forty-five minutes trying to calm an upset parent about a classroom issue, and the teacher has already left for the day. Can you resolve or solve the concern or situation now?

Lesson Learned

- Avoid answering late-afternoon telephone calls.

Resolutions

- Leave your office and go home.
- If the call is important, the individual will call again in the morning.

Strategy

- If you decide to answer, jot down key details. Handle the concern or issue in the morning.

THE HELPER

There are two sides to every story and TRUTH lays somewhere in the middle.
—Jean Gati

You are on your way to lunch, and three students are walking toward you. One of the students is visibly upset. You ask the young boy why he is crying. But before he can answer, his Little Florence Nightingale says in a sweet voice, *He's crying because I told him Robert is going to beat him up after school.* Robert is summoned to find out why he's threatening to beat up Mark. Once the two boys are together, you find out they're neighbors and friends. Robert is mad because Mark got him in trouble with the next-door neighbor. He wasn't really going to beat him up. He only wanted to scare Mark.

Lessons Learned

- Florence Nightingales or helpers make matters worse by carrying gossip.
- The real cause of disagreements between students may lie beneath the surface.

Resolutions

- Students apologized to each other.
- Mark moved out of state the following week. Some situations are resolved by life changes.

Strategies

- Investigate thoroughly and question all parties involved.
- Instruct key witnesses to write or dictate their statements and sign/date them.
- Listen carefully and take notes.
- Contact parents of the accused and victim.

TOMORROW IS ANOTHER DAY

I was always prepared for success but that means that I have to be prepared for failure too.—Shel Silverstein

Have you ever had days and moments when you felt things would be better if you could start your day over? Or take back something said or erase something written that was misinterpreted? While conducting a faculty meeting, you notice a teacher struggling to keep her eyes open. You speak to the teacher privately after the meeting and say, "You drive quite a distance in the mornings and probably get up very early to get here on time. I noticed you were having difficulty keeping your eyes open." You are blasted unexpectedly. "Are you accusing me of being an alcoholic? I am not drunk!"

Lessons Learned

- Sometimes good intentions are received inappropriately.
- Tomorrows are opportunities to revisit and repair.

Resolution

- Allow teachers time to calm down before attempting to clarify comments.

Strategy

- Tailor approaches and comments to meet staff personalities.

DEVELOP A THICK SKIN AND A FORGIVING HEART

It is better for a leader to make a mistake in forgiving than to make a mistake in punishing.—Muhammad

Conferences with staff members aren't always pleasant. Most school leaders support their teachers' decisions and actions wholeheartedly. There are times, however, when reported issues or concerns must be addressed and resolved. What do you do when during a conference, a staff member stands up, walks out of your office, and slams the door?

Lessons Learned

- Don't wear your feelings on your sleeve.
- Personal issues affect professional behavior and classroom performance.
- Time does heal hurts and wounds.

Resolutions

- Staff member apologized for the unprofessional behavior.
- Efforts were made to rebuild and repair the relationship.

Strategies

- Make a conscious effort to let go of hurts or slights.
- Readily forgive and move on.
- Don't hold grudges or seek revenge.
- Stay in tune with what is happening with staff professionally and personally.

DON'T THINK YOU'VE SEEN OR HEARD EVERYTHING

> *If we could sell our experiences for what they cost, we'd all be millionaires.—*
> Abigail Van Buren

You are suddenly greeted with a mixed group of students. You know something has happened just by the tones of their voices. A kindergartener was *mooned* by a third grader on the bus. You think to yourself, *What do these students know about mooning?* Surely, they are mistaken. Why would a student pull his or her pants down on the bus? During the interview, the kindergartener simply stated, "She pulled her pants down and showed me her butt!" The third grader's explanation for her action was she wanted to show the kindergartener what *mooning* meant. "My mother did the same thing when she was young as a joke."

Lessons Learned

- Sometimes the unbelievable is the truth.
- Keep an open mind.
- Parents should exercise caution sharing childhood antics.

Resolutions

- Student apologized to kindergartener.
- An appropriate consequence for the inappropriate behavior was implemented.
- Conference with parent.

Strategy

- Counsel parents if the opportunity presents itself.

LAUGH AT YOURSELF

If you could choose one characteristic that would get you through life, choose a sense of humor.—Jennifer Jones

Have you ever had any embarrassing moments such as slipping on a grape and falling in front of over two hundred students? Walking around the building with your top or shirt on the wrong side? A split seam in the back of your pants or losing a slip? Are you able to laugh at these embarrassing moments, or do you fret and worry? Embarrassing moments and the ability to laugh at yourself can add another dimension to your leadership. Your staff and students will see you *are* human. Also, they'll appreciate your sense of humor and ability to laugh at yourself.

Lessons Learned

- Laughter can take the sting out of unpleasant incidents.
- Develop a sense of humor to lighten situations.
- There's nothing wrong with being human.
- Most people laugh with you, not at you.

Resolutions

- Get over yourself.
- There is life after embarrassments.

Strategies

- Allow yourself to be human.
- Laugh louder and heartier than those who are laughing.
- Lighten up and enjoy the moment.

PROBLEMS DON'T ALWAYS HAVE SYMPTOMS

I have always grown from my problems and challenges, from the things that don't work out, that's when I really learned.—Carol Burnett

The school nurse is out sick today. Standing before you is a first grader who hurt her chin on the playground during recess. She is not crying or complaining about pain. You look inside her mouth and see a faint line of blood along her bottom gumline. The student asks to go to lunch with her class. Again, you inquire about pain, soreness, and whether she'll be able to eat. The student states her mouth is okay, it doesn't hurt, and she can eat. You check on the student after lunch. She's smiling and enjoying the activities in the classroom. The next morning you receive a phone call from the child's mother. Their dentist said her daughter's bottom teeth were pushed back a fraction of an inch not visible to the naked eye.

Lessons Learned

- Don't rely on what a child says about any injury.
- Some injuries don't cause physical symptoms.
- You can get hurt and experience pain later in the day or evening.

Resolutions

- Apologized to parent for incorrect judgment or action.
- Admitted mistake or bad call.

Strategies

- Put a policy in place to contact parents whenever a student is injured.
- Let parents decide the next step for injured students.

TEACHERS ARE PEOPLE TOO

While I know myself as a creation of God, I am also obligated to realize and remember that everyone else and everything else are also God's creation.—Maya Angelou

School administrators sometimes forget teachers are people too. They have insecurities, desires, aspirations, frailties, strengths, good days, and bad days. Behind every teacher is a person. Take the time to know your staff and their families. Knowing your faculty and staff will provide an avenue for connecting in a positive and meaningful way. Everyone wants to be accepted and respected for who they are regardless of their position or role. Cultivate a culture of caring and giving among your school staff and stakeholders. Show you care for the teacher as well as the person. Teachers who feel loved, safe, and secure will impart the same to their students.

Lessons Learned

- Simple random acts of kindness are powerful tools.
- Everyone wants to be recognized and appreciated.

Resolution

- Design and implement a recognition and appreciation plan for all stakeholders.

Strategies

- Recognize staff birthdays, anniversaries, and other milestones.
- Use cheerful smiles and greetings to brighten someone's day daily.
- Make a concerted effort to show your appreciation.
- Treat grade-level teams and office staff to lunch.
- Implement door prizes and drawings during staff meetings.

SOMETIMES THINGS ARE WHAT THEY SEEM

Trust your gut.—Barbara Walters

A class was heading out to recess after lunch one afternoon. As students entered the hall, they began holding their noses and complaining about an odor. *Someone stepped in dog mess!* Immediately students began checking the bottoms of their shoes. *Look over there!* On the floor was a little ball of human feces. Of course, since no one confessed to the deed, we were asked to solve the case.

Armed with a suggested time frame, we headed to the office to view our security camera footage. After watching several times, the assistant principal exclaimed, *He did it! Look! He's shaking his leg!* We watched the video again. Could this really be? Were our eyes deceiving us? Did we see what we thought we saw? There was a reason why he was shaking his leg in the footage. A confession from the student confirmed what was seen on the footage. This incident added a different meaning to the expression "shake a leg."

Lessons Learned

- Sometimes what appears or seems unlikely is.
- Cameras capture evidence as well as ensure safety.

Resolutions

- Student confessed to the deed.
- Parents sought medical help for their child.

Strategies

- Parent conference.
- Use available technology to resolve or solve issues or incidents.

THE SUB SANDWICH

Children may forget what you say, but they'll never forget how you make them feel.—Parker J. Palmer

Sitting outside your office is Tommy waiting to be seen. This is the fifth time this week you've met with him. He's a likeable boy, but for some reason Tommy and his fifth-grade teacher weren't getting along. Trying to find what will encourage him to behave in class has been an ongoing battle since the school year started. Today, however, instead of a mini lecture, you decide to try something different: treat Tommy to lunch for a week of *good behavior*. You've never tried this before, but what do you have to lose? Maybe a sub sandwich, a drink, and a bag of potato chips will open a new path.

During an open house event ten years later, a young man asks to speak with you for a few minutes. You step aside to have a private conversation with the young man in the hall. "I want to thank you for the sub sandwich you bought for me that day at your house." You suddenly realize who this young man is. Did his behavior change dramatically that school year? No, but communication and a special relationship developed and flourished throughout the remaining year.

Lessons Learned

- Be willing to try unconventional ideas or interventions.
- Results of actions or decisions may appear years later.
- Never underestimate the power of a kind word or deed.

Resolution

- Conferences with students became conversations, not lectures.

Strategy

- Use students' interests and hobbies to establish rapport for meaningful conversations.

WALK THE TALK

You have to set the tone and pace, define objectives and strategies, and demonstrate through personal example what you expect from others.—Stanley C. Gault

School administrators are walking billboards in their buildings. They are constantly scrutinized by staff, students, parents, and other stakeholders. Have you ever walked through a hall and a passing staff member asks if something is wrong? You're startled and surprised by the question. Your expression caused someone to misinterpret your state of mind. Be conscious of the influence your countenance and actions possess. Always demonstrate and model what you expect from others. For example, if you expect them to be respectful, courteous, polite, and kind, model. What you do and say speaks volumes.

Lessons Learned

- Facial expressions, actions, and words reflect the inner states of beings.
- Model what you expect.

Resolution

- Be conscious of your facial expressions and body language.

Strategies

- Do periodic mirror checks.
- Enlist an objective mentor for suggestions and feedback.

WHO MOVED MY CHEESE?

If you can't change your fate, change your attitude.—Amy Tan

Due to the lack of adequate funding, your school system will no longer offer music in elementary schools. Or, because of overcrowding in a neighboring school, you are receiving two hundred students and three new teachers the upcoming school year. These are examples of unexpected changes school leaders may have to face. Change is inevitable and happens to everyone. How principals handle change impacts their effectiveness as leaders in their buildings. Administrators who meet change with open minds see change as opportunities for innovative programs, school initiatives, and goals. Positive attitudes toward change create school cultures that encourage creative thinking among school staff.

Lessons Learned

- Changes can promote growth and new directions.
- Change can happen overnight.
- Positive attitudes provide and cultivate a unique perspective.

Resolutions

- Develop a mind-set that embraces change.
- Accept the inevitable as the nature of life.

Strategies

- Be factual and open by sharing the pros and cons of changes.
- Address any issues or concerns your staff may have with the change.
- Listen to staff and stakeholders with an open mind.
- Communicate how the change will impact your school and staff positively.
- Promote a *we can do this* attitude and lead the change effort.

PLAN WITH YOUR CLIENTELE IN MIND

My philosophy is that you can't do anything yourself. Your people have to do it.—Beth Pritchard

School leaders can't manage or lead schools by themselves. Nor are they in possession of every skill needed to run a successful school. Smart school administrators recognize this fact and make a concerted effort to use the strengths and skills of all faculty and staff to aid in accomplishing school initiatives and goals. How do administrators tap into the skills and expertise of staff members? They delegate. Relinquishing and delegating some of their responsibilities and tasks enables administrators to develop and cultivate leadership among staff within their building.

School administrators who don't use the talents and skills of staff weigh themselves down with tasks that can be performed by capable and competent teacher leaders. There is no better way to promote *buy-in* for new initiatives, programs, or changes than to involve the people who are responsible for implementing and maintaining school- and system-level curriculum or program initiatives. Administrators who are reluctant to utilize the strengths, talents, and skills of their faculty and staff may have a *me* rather than *we* mind-set. The *me* mind-set or attitude blocks divergent thinking and stunts the professional growth of everyone.

Lessons Learned

- Delegating does not lessen your role or authority in the building.
- You are not expected to be the master of all things.

Resolution

- Nurture and use the skills, talents, and strengths of school clientele.

Strategies

- Survey staff and stakeholders to assess their strengths, talents, and skills.
- Provide meaningful opportunities, tasks, and responsibilities to delegate.
- Schedule appropriate training to develop or expand the skillsets of potential teacher leaders.

HAPPY RETAINER HUNTING

Impossible situations can become possible miracles.—Robert H. Schuller

A tearful student comes to your office to let you know he accidently threw his retainer in the trash during lunch. He forgot to remove his retainer from the lunch tray. Lunch is over and all of the trash bags have been placed in the dumpster for pick up. *I will be in trouble if I don't find that retainer!* There are five large plastic bags filled with refuse in the dumpster. What are the chances of finding that retainer before dismissal time? Also, there are several reports laying on your desk needing immediate attention. Digging through trash in search of a tiny retainer is at the bottom of your agenda for the day, and besides, who wants to go through trash? What do you do?

Lessons Learned

- Doing what may be unpleasant can have a positive end.
- Miracles do happen.
- Students are more important than reports.
- There are always individuals willing to help.

Resolution

- Retainer was found.

Strategies

- Don a pair of rubber gloves and get to work.
- Enlist assistance of staff personnel along with the student.

SLAPPING-FACE TECHNIQUE

Bravery is the capacity to perform properly even when scared half to death.—
Omar N. Bradley

Every school administrator knows they can't be everywhere in the building at once. They expect faculty and staff to adhere to established policies, procedures, and expectations. Of course, no one has a perfect staff, and sometimes there are exceptions that must be handled. Everyone should strive to be their best and treat students in a respectful manner. If students are not treated appropriately, school administrators must be notified immediately. Staff struggle reporting incidents involving a colleague. No one likes to report an incident that may result in a reprimand or loss of a job. Staff should always do what is right for students and the school.

A staff member appears in your doorway and seems distraught and nervous. The individual pulls you aside and speaks in a muted voice. "A substitute teacher just slapped a student. This sub has been here before." The slap was witnessed, but the staff member was reluctant to say anything or tell you. The staff member decided to report the incident. Once school leaders receive a report, action is required. There is no time for hesitations or second thoughts. The safety and well-being of students and staff come first. School administration is not for the fainthearted.

Lessons Learned

- People do or try things that are not always conventional.
- Stand up for what is right and act despite fears.

Resolution

- Substitute was reprimanded and removed from the system's substitute list.

Strategies

- Encourage staff and faculty to report violations or improprieties immediately.
- Review system and school policies related to students and professional conduct periodically throughout the school year.

KNOCK ON THE OFFICE DOOR

No one is so brave that he is not disturbed by something unexpected. —Julius Caesar

The life of a school leader is filled with early morning knocks on office doors. Those knocks can be the harbinger of unexpected pleasant news or trying situations. Is there a teacher-staff conflict? Is a parent requesting a conference? Is a repair needed in the building? Is someone leaving because of her husband's new position or transfer? A myriad of questions float through your mind trying to guess the need of the person on the other side of the door. With much speculation and anticipation, you say, "Come in."

It's the new fourth grade teacher hired two weeks ago to fill an unexpected vacancy. You felt very fortunate to find another teacher so late in the school year. Everything seemed to be going well. The students and parents were happy. The new teacher worked well with her team. So, why is she handing you an envelope? "I am leaving my husband, and here's my resignation letter. Sorry, but I am packed and ready to go now." She turns, walks out, and closes the door. You sit holding the envelope in your hand staring at the closed office door. *What just happened?* You now have a class without a teacher, and school starts in an hour.

Lessons Learned

- Act even though there's a lump in your stomach.
- Life is full of the unexpected.
- No one is indispensable.
- Patience and persistence do pay off.
- You will survive.

Resolution

- Place a capable substitute in the class until a new teacher is hired.

Strategies

- Enlist the help of your staff and colleagues when recruiting personnel.
- Contact local colleges and universities for names of recent graduates.

SELF-MADE HERO

> *Anyone can possess, anyone can profess, but it is an altogether different thing to confess.*—Shannon L. Adler

An email from a teacher requires your immediate attention. A student reported seeing *bomb in school* written on the wall in the boys' restroom. Several weeks ago, a neighboring middle school had to evacuate their building twice because of bomb threats written on the walls in restrooms. For the safety of all involved, students were evacuated while first responders checked the building to ensure safety. You must investigate to find who wrote the message on the wall to cover all bases. This is just what you need on Friday afternoon two hours before dismissal. You start with the student who reported the incident and check for other possible suspects.

Next, secure samples of the suspects' handwritings and include a sample of the student who was first on the scene. Several teachers help to compare the collected writing samples with a photo picture of the writing on the wall. Each person evaluates the sample writings and selects one that matches the original. Sometimes, if there isn't a need for an immediate decision or action, review everything again with a fresh pair of eyes and clearer mind early in the morning. By doing so, any additional evidence that appears the next day can be considered. Parents are not contacted until the right suspect is found.

Lessons Learned

- Children have a fervent desire to be recognized.
- Praise students and adults for making the right choices.
- Turn bad choices into memorable life lessons for students, if applicable.

Resolution

- The student reporter wrote the message and confessed. He wanted to be called a hero.
- Student was assigned an appropriate consequence for his action.

- Student apologized for his action.
- A parent conference was held.

Strategy

- Take your time and be thorough when investigating incidents.

THE SLIDE RIDE

> *When all things go bad, do not think so badly about all things, instead think about the things that made all things bad and change something!*—Ernest Agyemang Yeboah

You hang up your office phone in disbelief. A parent called to inform you about an incident that occurred on the playground during afternoon recess. Her son's arm was broken during a ride down the slide. The son said the teacher gave them foil to sit on so they could slide faster. He fell coming down the slide. You're questioning what the student told his mother. This teacher has never done anything unsafe or harmful for students. You politely thank the parent for the information and say you'll discuss the matter with the teacher.

As you walk down the hall to the teacher's classroom, you think to yourself, *Surely this parent is mistaken. Why would someone do something like that? Luckily, the parent isn't going to press charges against the school and the teacher. The teacher will have a perfectly good explanation for me to share with the mother. Whoever heard of someone going down a sliding board on foil?* After sharing your conversation with the teacher, you are shocked by the teacher's reply. "Oh, I do that with my own children. Foil makes their ride down the sliding board faster, and it's so much fun. I wouldn't intentionally hurt any of my students."

Lessons Learned

- Your best teachers can also make bad choices.
- Good intentions can have negative or adverse results.

Resolution

- Teacher apologized to parent and offered restitution for the doctor's bill.

Strategies

- Accept the fact that the unexpected can happen in any situation.

- Learn from the unexpected outcomes and make positive changes.

THE LUNCH BOX

Trust instinct to the end, even though you can give no reason. —Ralph Waldo Emerson

"I can't find my lunch box, and I know I had it when I came in the building this morning."

How many times have you heard this claim? Book bags, backpacks, hats, coats, sweaters, and books. Somehow, they all manage to show up in unlikely places. This young student is very upset. The only way to get him to calm down is to join the search. Offering to help did stop the tears. So, steps are retraced, and the entire building is searched inside and out. No lunch box is found. Your instinct is saying maybe he didn't bring a lunch box to school today. Did someone mistakenly take his lunch box for theirs? This happens quite often in a school.

You send the student back to class and continue checking the building. Upon returning to your office, the parent is called. After briefly giving his mother an update on the morning event, she offers to check the house and car. A few minutes pass by and his mother returns to the phone. The lunch box is on the back seat of the car. Evidently, he hurried out of the car and left his lunch box. He *thought* he had brought his lunch box into the building.

Lessons Learned

- Trust your instincts.
- Sometimes a possibility becomes the reality.

Resolution

- The lost lunchbox was found.

Strategy

- Be open to unusual ways that problems or situations can be resolved.

MISSING FUNDS

Any time you suffer a setback or disappointment, put your head down and plow ahead. —Les Brown

You have just finished a private conversation with one of your P.T.O. officers. Funds are missing from their account. A relatively large amount of money has been withdrawn over the summer to purchase personal items. Bank statements show items purchased were personal, not school related. The only person with access to the card over the summer was the P.T.O. president. Unfortunately, due to a job transfer, she's no longer in the area. You are devastated by the news and withdrawal of school funds.

The former officer was well liked and a champion for your students, teachers, parents, and school. Are you a poor judge of character? Did you miss telling signs? How can anyone intentionally misuse funds raised for students and teachers? Will the school ever recover from this inappropriate act? Will we be able to collect the missing funds from the individual?

Lessons Learned

- You can't predict or control what other people do.
- You can and do recover from unpleasant situations or incidents.
- The only person you can effectively control is yourself.

Resolution

- Parent/officer replaced the missing funds.

Strategies

- Require two signatures on checks.
- Debit card for P.T.O./P.T.A. account isn't needed.
- Secure P.T.O./P.T.A. books and checks in school's vault whenever school is not in session.

PLAYING HOOKY

You don't always win your battles, but it's good to know you fought. —John Greenleaf Whittier

The Young brothers aren't here today. Several students reported they hid from the bus and went back home. They really don't need to miss any more days of school. Neither one of them is strong academically. They're new to your school this year and seem to be having trouble adjusting to this school environment and area. One eyewitness said the boys ducked down behind a sign and waited until the bus pulled off from the bus stop. They may be roaming around the neighborhood. We need to contact their mother at work to let her know what happened. You are already visualizing your school on the front page of the local newspaper.

After much consternation and worry, a phone call from the mother eases your mind. She found the boys in the house eating cereal and watching cartoons. Mom said the boys stated they *missed* the bus. You inform the mother that according to students who were at the bus stop, the boys hid from the bus and were outside in time to be picked up for school. The mother continues to insist they didn't miss the bus on purpose. Do you repeat what several eyewitnesses told you? Is it going to change their mother's mind? You now know where the brothers are. They are safe and sound.

Lessons Learned

- Don't continue to beat a dead horse.
- Pick your battles.
- Know when to pull back and move on.

Resolution

- The missing boys were located.

Strategies

- Focus on what really is important for the situation.
- Seek win-win solutions for all parties involved.

THE FIVE-DOLLAR LUNCH BOX

It is the Holy Spirit's job to convict, God's job to judge and my job to love.—Billy Graham

You can hardly believe you spent forty-five minutes on the phone talking with an irate parent about a five-dollar lunch box left on the bus. The parent is insisting—no, demanding—some action be taken, or she'll contact the Board of Education and superintendent about your unwillingness to cooperate. How many times have you heard this empty threat during the run of a day? You don't have any control over what is left on the bus nor what happens on the bus. Is this fuss even necessary or warranted? Perhaps contacting the bus driver will satisfy this mother's ridiculous demand. Why is it your responsibility to replace the missing lunch box if it isn't found? Who left the lunch box on the bus?

Contacting the bus driver didn't satisfy the parent. A call was made to the superintendent. You've been directed to resolve the issue as soon as possible.

You're reminded that we are here to serve the public. The lunch box was not on the bus. You can't believe that a five-dollar lunch box would cause so much trouble and reach the office of the superintendent. As much as you don't want to, you call the parent and express your willingness to work with her to resolve the issue. You find out the mother recently became a single parent and is struggling financially as a single mother. Losing that lunch box meant a lot to her situation. You now have another perspective.

Lesson Learned

- What is not important to you may be important to others.

Resolution

- Parent was reimbursed for lost lunch box.

Strategy

- Be willing to view a situation from another person's perspective.

THE GLASSES

Apology is not about saying I'm sorry, but it is all about the meaning you put behind the apology and admitting that you are the wrong party.—Unarine Ramaru

"So, you can't find your glasses. They were left on your desk before going out for recess. Your teacher checked everywhere in the classroom, and you checked outside. Well, the custodian checked the playground again and didn't see a pair of glasses anywhere outside. I'll contact your parents and let them know what we've done here to find the missing glasses. Maybe they will turn up somewhere soon."

"Mrs. Jones, we've looked everywhere for your son's glasses and have not been able to find them. He said they were left on his desk before he went outside to play. We have been unable to locate the glasses. Mrs. Jones, is it possible he may have left them home today thinking he had his glasses? We have searched everywhere." Of course, the mother insists that if her son said he left his glasses on the desk, then that's what he did. He does not make mistakes. The school will just replace his new $150.00 pair of glasses if they aren't found.

Lessons Learned

- There are some people who will apologize when wrong.
- Keep having faith and belief in people no matter the circumstance.

Resolutions

- The glasses were found in the student's backpack.
- Parent called and apologized for her inappropriate comments and behavior.

Strategy

- Maintain a positive attitude and professional manner with all situations.

THE DEVIL MADE ME DO IT

It is better to offer no excuse than a bad one.—George Washington

School administrators listen to a variety of explanations for wrong choices and inappropriate actions from children and adults. From time to time, a few explanations are noteworthy and possible candidates for a *Ripley's Believe It or Not* category. When they appear, take a deep breath, keep your composure, and remain calm. Remember, this too will pass. Sometimes when you are trying to resolve an issue or determine who is telling the truth, it isn't easy to maintain a professional and composed demeanor. It is especially hard when you are attempting to obtain the truth between an adult and a student.

A paraprofessional brings a student to your office for disrespectful behavior and not following instructions. The student accompanying the paraprofessional has a known behavior problem and has difficulty following directions given by adults. After listening to the rendition of the incident described by the adult, the student declares, "She hit me!" The paraprofessional claims she didn't hit him. "You were disrespectful!" Both are equally passionate with their responses. Knowing the student's current history of misbehavior, you know the student probably did behave as described. The following morning you are greeted with an unannounced visit from the student's mother, who believes her son.

Lessons Learned

- Don't base judgments and decisions on past behaviors.
- If something doesn't feel right, something is wrong.
- Adults try to cover their inappropriate actions too.

Resolutions

- Staff member admitted inappropriate behavior toward student.
- Apology to parent by staff member and administrator.

Strategies

- Willingly admit misjudgments.
- Acknowledge and accept the possibility of human failings, and forgive.

THE RELUCTANT PATIENT

You can pretend that bad things will never happen. But life is a lot easier if you realize and admit that sometimes they do.—Lois Lowry

No school administrator has a school consisting of perfect faculty and staff. As a matter of fact, it is unrealistic for anyone to expect perfection. It is the responsibility of leaders to provide professional development activities or resources to help their staff grow professionally and personally under their leadership. Your school clientele are people too and may experience people problems such as divorce, emotional instability, loss, health concerns, alcohol, and drug abuse. Some situations or issues are easier to handle or address than others. What if you have reason to suspect alcohol or drug abuse?

This is the second early morning conference with Ms. Smith, and there is a strong odor of mouthwash emanating from the classroom. Why would anyone use that much mouthwash? You spoke to Ms. Smith three weeks ago about your suspicions and recommended contacting the school system's employee assistance program for help and support. Is Ms. Smith still following the recommendations of the program? Why are you still smelling mouthwash? Does she not realize the consequence of her actions? You can't look the other way or talk yourself out of doing what you know is the next step.

Lessons Learned

- Problematic decisions build and strengthen character.
- Executing a difficult action is easier when it's the right decision or correct action.
- There are individuals who do not accept responsibility for their behavior.

Resolution

- Staff was referred for further disciplinary action.
- Staff member resigned.

Strategies

- Do what is right regardless of the circumstance and its difficulty.
- Document all actions taken and resources used.
- Always put children first.

DISSATISFIED CUSTOMERS

There is only one way to avoid criticism: do nothing, say nothing, and be nothing.—Aristotle

Every school leader, regardless of their years of experience and effectiveness, encounters a parent, teacher, or concerned citizen who is never satisfied with any policies, procedures, instructional initiatives, or programs occurring in their building. Despite conferences and meetings held allowing them to express their ideas and suggestions, they continually bombard you and the office staff with issues and negative comments. Closing your door to disgruntled customers sends the wrong message. Handling unsupportive clients in a professional manner fosters and encourages creative problem solving that promotes buy-in.

Lessons Learned

- Trying to please everyone pleases no one in the end.
- Guard your integrity at all cost.
- Being liked is not equal to doing what's right.

Resolution

- Listen with an open and nonjudgmental mind.

Strategies

- Consider ideas, suggestions, and recommendations aligned with school and system goals.
- Treat clientele respectfully.

THE UNEXPECTED

It is strange how new and unexpected conditions bring out unguessed ability to meet them.—Edgar Rice Burroughs

School leaders are proud of their ability to handle situations and incidents that arise during the run of a school day. Over time, principals develop an arsenal of tools, strategies, and techniques to help them address inappropriate behavior or wrong choices. There are times when they are confronted with a behavior that is unusual and unexpected. Incidents of this nature must be handled on a case-by-case basis. Also, there are strategies that are more effective with younger children and unsuccessful with older children. Therefore, it is very important for principals to align their technique or strategy with the appropriate developmental age of their students.

A second grader is reported for urinating during Extended Daycare recess the previous afternoon. This is not an incident that has occurred before, and you're wondering the best method for resolving this situation. The student has never been referred to the office for inappropriate behavior or wrong choices. Should his parents be contacted and told about the incident? How can you maintain a student's dignity and have a meaningful conference? After several moments of weighing different approaches and interventions, you conduct a conference with the student to help him choose a better course of action for school in the future.

Lessons Learned

- Utilize unconventional techniques occasionally to achieve your objective.
- Present students with the opportunity to correct their behavior.

Resolution

- Student confessed, apologized, and never repeated the behavior during recess.

Strategies

- Encourage student participation in problem solving whenever it's appropriate.
- Use a variety of interventions and techniques to promote behavior self-regulation.

FAMILY FEUD

Families and their problems go on and they aren't solved, they're dealt with.
—Roger Ebert

Families of today consist of a variety of combinations and states. The percentage of intact two-parent families is dwindling as single-parent and blended families rise. Regardless of the family makeup, disagreements among the adults can spill into the school on occasion and cause disruption and confusion. School administrators often find themselves thrust in the middle of custody battles, separations, divorces, kidnapping attempts, and grandparent issues. Often classroom teachers, students, and the office staff are pulled into the family tugs-of-war that impact everyone. School leaders must focus on the school's role and maintain order.

It's parent orientation night and everything seems to be going well. Suddenly, you receive a radio message requesting your presence immediately. An altercation was broken up between an ex-husband and the new boyfriend by another parent who happened to be in the area at the time. A preK child being held by the boyfriend hit his head on the wall during the shoving match between the two men. By the time you arrive, the ex-husband who initiated the fight was nowhere in sight. He fled the building. You stand there in disbelief while gathering facts from the parent who intervened. Nothing of this magnitude has happened at prior parent meetings or gatherings.

Lessons Learned

- Act quickly and professionally when unexpected events occur.
- How you react and respond to a situation is just as important as handling the situation.

Resolution

- Conferences were held with both families.
- Guidelines and protocols for future parent involvement visits were implemented for the families.
- Supervised school visits were established for the ex-wife's significant other.

Strategies

- Gather facts and written statements from all witnesses as soon as possible when incidents occur.
- Instruct staff to notify you of potential family situations.
- Circulate, monitor, and be present at all school-related functions and activities.
- Request the presence of a school resource police officer during school functions, if needed.

ANXIOUS HELICOPTER PARENTS

Anxiety does not empty tomorrow of its sorrows, but empties today of its strength.—Charles Spurgeon

All administrators have experienced or dealt with helicopter parents. No matter how effectively and efficiently administrators operate their schools and manage staff, they will have that parent who is fearful or worried about their child's or children's well-being during the instructional day. They tend to linger in the halls and constantly question and inquire about all aspects of the school's instructional programs, policies, and classroom practices. They also are a source of frustration and anxiety for their children's teachers, who can't seem to provide the classroom environment needed to support their children's intellectual development and curiosity.

Parents who hover cause more harm than good. Their overbearing presence and pressure for their children to achieve often impacts social and emotional development. Also, helicopter parents limit or impede the ability of their children to develop appropriate problem-solving and coping skills. Children will experience disappointments, setbacks, and possibly failures throughout their academic career and life. No one wants children and youth to struggle, but it is necessary for them to learn and acquire strategies, techniques, and life skills to help them be resilient. Dealing with overprotective parents is not an easy task for school leaders.

Lessons Learned

- The source of helicopter parents' overprotectiveness stems from their past experiences.
- Parents want to shield children from disappointments, hurts, and struggles.

Resolution

- Conference with parents to relieve the situation if the teacher and student are at risk in class.

Strategies

- Listen and exercise patience and understanding.
- Be transparent and respond to questions or concerns to relieve anxiety and overprotectiveness.
- Encourage parents to serve as volunteers to assist in their transitioning in a new school and grade level.

A JOY OF MOTHERHOOD: BREASTFEEDING

Whatever you do, you need courage. Whatever course you decide upon there is always someone to tell you are wrong. There are always difficulties arising that tempt you to believe your critics are right.—Ralph Waldo Emerson

There are some things that are viewed as sacred in our country, such as mothers, apple pie, and baseball. Saying or doing anything about these icons may bring the wrath of many upon you. Mothers breastfeeding is another sacred activity of our society. But is there an appropriate way to breastfeed in public? What if baby decides he or she is hungry in the middle of a Mother's Day program at school? A mother, responding to the cries of her little one, literally pulls out a breast and begins feeding her baby. The mother continues watching the program, ignoring stares and whispers from other parents sitting nearby.

You can't ignore the eyes and motions from parents to get your attention. Also, you know you're in an impossible situation. No matter what you decide, someone will criticize your actions. The mother is not going to be happy when asked to cover her breast. There probably will be a posting on Facebook stating the principal is against breastfeeding that very afternoon. Do you ignore the stares and hope the baby finishes eating soon, or act?

Lessons Learned

- Regardless of fear of criticism, act on what you feel is right.
- Accept with grace negative comments or outcomes.
- Facing fears increases courage.

Resolution

- Mother angrily complied with the request to cover her breast.

Strategies

- Remain calm and in control.
- Be polite and respectful.
- Choose your words carefully when handling a potentially volatile situation.

THE BRIGHT YELLOW DRESS

No-pocket jeans are only slightly less irritating than thong underwear.—Patricia Briggs

Something is causing quite a stir in your lunchroom. Several staff members have asked if you saw what the new lunchroom volunteer had on. Everyone is talking about it, but of course, no one is saying anything to the volunteer. She's wearing a bright yellow dress without a slip underneath. The main problem, however, is that the black thong worn by the parent is visible through the dress. Naturally, you are expected to be the one to let the volunteer know her underwear is showing. Are you the only person that could have pulled the parent aside and spoken privately about the dress? No. Is that your job as the school leader?

Lessons Learned

- Embarrassing and delicate things will be passed to you.
- You acquire skills handling sensitive situations.
- Sincerity and forthrightness are appreciated.
- Don't assume all actions are intentional.

Resolution

- Parent volunteer was unaware her underwear was visible through the dress.
- Parent volunteer went home, changed attire, and returned.
- Parent volunteer apologized and continued to help in the school.

Strategies

- Be professional and nonjudgmental.
- Speak in a positive and supportive manner.
- Be open to listening to explanations.
- Be forgiving.

UNREQUITED YOUNG LOVE

Unrequited love is a ridiculous state, and it makes those in it behave ridiculously.—Cassandra Clare

It is said that there is no love like young love. It is exciting, mysterious, and heartwarming. What about young "love" that occurs in fourth grade and is unrequited? Not only can this love be one-sided, but it can also disrupt a classroom and cause anxiety for a fourth-grade girl. There were endless notes, unwanted gifts, and stares from a classmate who evidently had a serious crush. The boy was quiet, consistent, and determined to express his affection. The girl's refusal and obvious lack of interest did not dissuade the student's quest for her attention in class. He obtained everyone's attention by bequeathing his penis upon death to show the depth of his love.

Lessons Learned

- Students' rights need to be considered and honored.
- Children occasionally say surprising things.

Resolution

- Conference with parents of both students.
- Student was moved to another room per parent request.

Strategies

- Be approachable and ready to listen.
- Respect the feelings of all students.

DEATH WISH

> *There are some people who should stay quiet, because they understand. As there are those that should stay quiet because they don't understand. Somethings are better left unsaid or voiced.*—Anthony Liccione

Early mornings are hectic in most schools and homes. Forgotten homework, lost lunch money, spill in the cafeteria, a fallen ceiling tile, no substitute for a teacher, or a late bus arrival are examples of unexpected situations school leaders may face on school mornings. Parents probably handle situations at home or on the way to school that dampen spirits and cause tempers to rise. School leaders make every effort to remain calm when issues or situations arise. There is no need to get upset over something that you have no control over. Children rely on parents and other significant adults in their lives to be loving, caring, and understanding.

A student exiting his father's car was visibly upset and on the verge of tears. When asked what was wrong, he replied, "My dad said he wished I was dead." Who would say that to a child?

Lessons Learned

- There are children who are handicapped by their parents.
- Do whatever you can to brighten a child's day in your span of control.
- Be positive and supportive.

Resolution

- Teacher was informed about the incident.
- Student was referred to the school counselor.

Strategies

- Focus on students' facial expressions and body language.
- Build relationships with students, parents, and staff.
- Keep teachers abreast of known family situations or dynamics.

SOILED TOILET SEAT

We need to understand the difference between discipline and punishment. Punishment is what you do to someone; discipline is what you do for someone.—Zig Ziglar

You look up from your desk and see a young student standing before you with his classroom teacher. After using the restroom, he wiped feces on the toilet seat in the boys' restroom. There is no question about who soiled the toilet seat because the student admitted doing the act. After conferencing with the student about his action, you contact his mother and inform them of the incident and your consequence for his behavior. The mother isn't pleased with the consequence but couldn't invalidate your decision.

Lesson Learned

- Consequences for misbehavior need to be age appropriate and aligned with the infraction.

Resolution

- Provided a pair of rubber gloves and a bucket of warm, soapy water, the student cleaned the feces off the toilet seat.

Strategies

- Employ a witness for potentially sensitive situations.
- Explain the rationale for consequences for inappropriate behaviors.
- Be consistent, reasonable, and fair.

ALTERING BIRTH DATE FOR KINDERGARTEN ENROLLMENT

Lying is a deliberate choice to mislead a target without giving any notification of the intent to do so. There are two major forms of lying, concealment leaving out true information; and falsification, or presenting false information as if it were true. —Paul Ekman

Parents wait eagerly for information about kindergarten registration. They can hardly wait to enroll little Johnnie or Susie for kindergarten. For many students, kindergarten is the first experience in a school. There are, however, states with a specific age requirement to enter kindergarten. Some children who don't meet the age requirement must wait until the following year to enter school. This is a frustrating predicament for many parents. They try to find loopholes or assessments to enable them to enroll their children without meeting the age requirement for kindergarten. In one instance, altering a birth date solved the problem.

Lessons Learned

- There are individuals who do whatever is necessary to get their way.
- Consequences of actions can become apparent in the future.

Resolution

- The alteration was discovered, and appropriate action was taken.

Strategies

- Direct office staff to check records carefully.
- Act immediately if you suspect false information.

SMILE! CANDID CAMERA

Character is doing the right thing when nobody is looking. There are too many people who think that the only thing that is wrong is to get caught. —J. C. Watts

An angry and upset parent calls and reports the inappropriate behavior of her son's bus driver. "He was rude and doesn't know what he is doing! He needs to be fired. I want him reported to the transportation director. I can't believe how he spoke to me." You calmly assure the parent that you will report her concerns to the transportation director as soon as possible. If the mother's alleged claims are true, the bus driver will be handled immediately. Later that day you receive a phone call from the transportation director. He has viewed the video on the bus and gained a unique perspective on the parent's allegations against the bus driver.

The parent was unaware of cameras on the bus to help monitor student bus behavior and bus safety. The parent ended up apologizing to the bus driver and transportation director for her behavior and use of profanity on the bus.

Lessons Learned

- Don't assume everyone is truthful about their actions.
- Obtain both sides of a story before you make any decisions.

Resolution

- Parent apologized to bus driver and transportation director.

Strategies

- Obtain all pertinent facts about an incident.
- Utilize all equipment and resources available to assess a situation.

MY GRANDSON DOESN'T CUSS

You've always had a good grasp on what's right and wrong. You just have a hard time admitting that sometimes you choose the wrong.—Jessica Sorensen

We all have experienced that parent or grandparent who has excuses for their son or daughter's misbehavior regardless of what it is. The frustrating thing about the situation is the child is aware and uses this *power* and *support* whenever possible. School administrators and teachers have difficulty convincing unbelieving parents and grandparents their children aren't perfect and are subject to making wrong choices and misbehaving. A school leader's and teacher's word are second to their children's word. Parents and grandparents who perceive their children as being perfect usually have a day of reckoning.

Tommy was reported for sassing the bus driver and using profanity on the way home from school. During a telephone conference, grandmother insists the bus driver must be mistaken and has confused her grandson with another student on the bus. She emphatically says her grandson doesn't use cuss words and is respectful to adults. You don't dispel the grandmother's claims but invite her to view the bus video in your office that afternoon.

46   *Chapter 2*

Lessons Learned

- Things do come to light in due time.
- Let the proof be in the pudding.
- Don't argue with closed minds.
- Some closed minds are opened in unique ways.

Resolution

- Grandmother viewed the bus video and disciplined her grandson.
- The student was suspended from riding the bus.

Strategies

- Be patient and calm.
- Choose your battles.

THE UNEXPECTED VISITOR

> *I was just about to open the door when it opened up right in front of me. And there stood my parents. Is there a word for that moment when two parties are so equally shocked to see each other given the circumstances that all they can do is stare at each other open mouthed?*—August Westman

You've been called down to this kindergarten classroom numerous times this week. Mary continues to cause havoc in the room. She throws whatever is within hands' reach and runs around the classroom at will. There doesn't seem to be any cause for her erratic behavior. At this point, nothing seems to work. A day or two at home has not made a difference. As a matter of fact, Mary returns after missing school more determined to create chaos in the class and interrupt the learning of others.

Grandfather, who works nearby, decides to visit his only granddaughter one afternoon. You escort him down to the classroom hoping everything is calm and peaceful. Mary's grandfather peers through the window before opening the classroom door. He stops and says, "Oh my!" Mary is throwing balls of paper around the classroom. Grandfather opens the door. Mary stops and stands with her mouth open, dropping the paper in her hand. "Grandpa!" The room became quiet.

Lesson Learned

- Never underestimate the power of a surprise visit.

Resolutions

- Grandfather began to *drop in* regularly to check on his granddaughter's behavior.
- A Behavior Management Plan was implemented incorporating grandfather's visits.
- Mary's behavior improved as she earned positive rewards with her grandfather.

Strategies

- Be open to trying unusual strategies.
- Involve significant family members as integral parts of Behavior Management Plans.
- Determine which interventions work with individual students.
- Persevere.

GREEN APPLE WINE COOLER

The truth will sooner come out of error than confusion.—Francis Bacon

You are radioed to come to the cafeteria for an unusual situation. You hurry to the cafeteria wondering what the situation may be. You know anything is possible during lunch and hope for the best. A group of fifth-grade students are gathered around a student who claims something is wrong with the bottle of water in his lunch box. It doesn't taste right and smells funny. A student sitting next to the fifth grader with the "bad" water states, "It smells like a green apple wine cooler." The student starts to cry. "I thought it was water." You send the student through the serving line to buy a bottle of water. This is a first.

Lessons Learned

- Consider circumstances and the age of students when deciding on an action.
- What you may think is impossible may just be possible.

Resolutions

- Parents of fifth grader were contacted immediately.
- Student's older brother put the clear green apple wine cooler in a water bottle.
- The fifth grader did not receive a consequence for the error and confusion.

- Parents were apologetic and appreciated how the water incident was handled.

Strategies

- Contact parents immediately for serious incidents or situations.
- Follow the spirit of a school policy, if applicable.
- Consider the intent and age of the student to determine the appropriate consequence.
- Allow parents to handle what is in their sphere of control.

STOLEN CELL PHONE

> *If children learn of sex as a relation between their parents to which they owe their own existence, they learn of it in its best form and in connection with its biological purpose.* —Bertrand Russell

You are headed to a teacher's classroom in response to a request for an administrator. When you arrive, the teacher is standing at the entrance of her classroom with an object in her hand. It's a cell phone. She has just confiscated a stolen cell phone from a student in the classroom. It's not the stolen cell phone that warranted your immediate presence. It's what the student downloaded that was a distraction during language arts class and caught the teacher's attention. The student was viewing explicit pictures from a pornography site. The cell phone had been taken from one of his classmates.

Lessons Learned

- Expect the unexpected when working in a school.
- Sensitive topics and situations require extreme calmness.

Resolutions

- The cell phone was removed from the classroom.
- Parents of the students were contacted.
- Student was assigned out-of-school suspension.
- Parents sought outside professional assistance.

Strategies

- Encourage teachers to always monitor students periodically during class.
- Teachers must arrange students to enable visibility of computer and/or Chromebook screens.

- Direct teachers to contact a school administrator if they suspect inappropriate behavior or use of equipment.

BOXING OR SELF-DEFENSE LESSONS

School leaders face many challenges and unexpected issues daily. They usually rise to situations when confronted with professionalism and wisdom. There is no problem too hard to tackle or overcome. They stand and fight for students' and teachers' rights. School administrators must remain focused and poised for action. They are willing to handle whatever is placed before them. What do you do if a parent threatens to beat your butt because you took her son's iPad? The parent is on her way and will arrive in fifteen minutes. Should you head to the gym and get a quick mini lesson on self-defense from the P.E. coach?

Lessons Learned

- Tough situations strengthen your resolve about issues.
- Pray for a calm spirit before confronting upset or disgruntled individuals.
- Never let them see you sweat.
- Time calms ruffled spirits.

Resolutions

- Parent had an unforeseen emergency and canceled trip to the school.
- Parent picked up son's iPad the following day without any difficulty.

Strategies

- Remain emotionally calm when facing volatile circumstances.
- Stand behind policies and procedures established for unauthorized items brought to school.

SASSING MOM

A child who is allowed to be disrespectful to his parents will not have true respect for anyone.—Billy Graham

You've been trying to schedule a conference with Bobby's mother for several weeks. Finally, you have been able to get his mother to come to the school after numerous attempts. Bobby and his mother are escorted into the conference room. The session is going well until Bobby begins sassing his mother and responding in a rude manner when addressed. You sit there amazed

50   *Chapter 2*

because you haven't experienced this type of behavior from Bobby. Do you say something to Bobby about his rude behavior? His mother appears to allow the unacceptable behavior. Bobby is *her* son. What do you do?

Lessons Learned

- Do what you know is right.
- Expect respectful behavior from everyone.

Resolutions

- The meeting was stopped momentarily.
- The student was reprimanded for his disrespectful behavior.
- Student apologized to his mother.
- The meeting resumed without additional disrespectful remarks or inappropriate behavior from the student.
- Principal designed a Behavior Management Plan between school and home for the parent.

THE COMPLIMENT

Remember not only to say the right thing in the right place, but far more difficult still, to leave unsaid the wrong thing at the tempting moment.—Benjamin Franklin

Mrs. B is wanting her son placed in another kindergarten teacher's classroom. She doesn't feel the present teacher meets her son's needs. As far as you know, there hasn't been any prior concerns expressed by Mrs. B. You're puzzled about this unexpected requested conference and have no idea what to expect or how to prepare. The best thing to do is to listen closely, take notes, and try to resolve the situation. Mrs. B takes a seat and says without hesitation, "The teacher said my son wrapped his arms around her like a little monkey. She called him a monkey!" The teacher is Caucasian, and the student is African American.

Lessons Learned

- There are some thoughts that are best not said.
- Don't assume everyone can communicate with culturally diverse students and parents.
- What is intended as a compliment may not be received as a compliment.

Resolutions

- Scheduled a conference with the teacher and parent.
- Met with the teacher and explained why the student's mother was upset.
- The student remained in his current classroom.
- No additional incidents of this nature occurred for the remainder of the year.

Strategies

- Provide professional learning for faculty on cultural diversity.
- Periodically monitor and assess the effectiveness of communication in your building with all stakeholders.

HUGS MAKE THE WORLD GO AROUND

One of the most courageous decisions you'll ever make is finally letting go of what is hurting your heart and soul.—Brigitte Nicole

A teacher walks into your office visibly upset. Tears are running down her face. You ask, "What's the matter?" The teacher states that a parent in her class has forbidden hugs. The parent didn't provide a reason but was emphatic about her daughter not being touched by the teacher. This request is surprising to both of you. "Students hug me all the time. They walk up to me after recess or greet me in the morning with a hug. Her daughter hugs me every day. I care about my students. I am a teacher. Do I turn away when she tries to hug me? What do I do?"

Lesson Learned

- Behavior and attitudes are shaped by past experiences.

Resolutions

- The teacher abided by the parent's request.
- Student stopped hugging the teacher per mother's instructions.
- Parent was victimized and abused as a child.

CHAPTER 2 SUMMARY

School administrators confront and address a variety of issues, concerns, and incidents involving students, staff, parents, and other stakeholders. School systems have adopted student codes of conduct, board policies, rules, and regulations outlining guidelines and procedures for handling situations as they arise. Principals often use a variety of strategies, interventions, and techniques to handle usual and unusual school-related incidents. School administrators are exposed to other situations and their resolutions. These additional scenarios provided will extend current repertoires of interventions, techniques, and strategies used to address and resolve school clientele matters.

GOING DEEPER

Time to Reflect

1. Are there any situations, incidents, or events presented in chapter 2 that you've addressed or experienced in your school?
2. What lesson or lessons have you learned from experiences or incidents in your building?
3. Are there any situations you would handle differently in the future? If so, what situations will you handle differently? Briefly explain why.
4. What strategies, techniques, and interventions were very effective for you?
5. Why were the strategies, techniques, and interventions effective? Jot down your thoughts.
6. Do you feel equipped to handle discipline problems in your school?
7. What resources or personnel are available to assist you with challenging student behaviors?
8. Do you have a school-wide Behavior Management Plan?
9. How often do you discuss discipline and your behavior expectations with faculty and staff?
10. Are you familiar with your school system's Code of Conduct for students?
11. Share strategies and/or interventions you use with a school leader colleague or mentor. What is their perspective?
12. Develop a portfolio of effective strategies and techniques for improving classroom management and student misbehavior for your building.

Chapter Three

Time and Energy Stealers

Maintaining High-Maintenance Problem Personnel

> *I think different people have different problems and different relations to the exhibition of their work.*—Richard Serra

One of the biggest challenges all school administrators face is managing and supervising staff. Getting everyone to work as a team focused on their school's goals or initiatives is not an easy feat. Buildings are comprised of a variety of people with different personalities, skills, talents, and levels of effectiveness. School leaders must become proficient at balancing time, energy, and resources to maintain and ensure highly effective staff. Time and focus become critical factors for administrators who want a positive impact on students' academic achievement and school goals. An unwavering focus is needed to help personnel requiring additional instructional support.

Every school has personnel in their organization that tend to drain other fellow colleagues emotionally, socially, and professionally. They demand or gain attention from school leaders and staff through their inappropriate behaviors, inadequacies, personalities, and lack of judgment. It is the responsibility of administrators to monitor and supervise school personnel. Helping staff increase their effectiveness as classroom teachers is a continuous process that entails assessing staff needs and providing appropriate resources to promote growth. Addressing staff needs may pull school administrators from other important tasks and functions as instructional leaders.

To respond to ever-changing cries for continuous academic growth, quality teachers, and school improvement, principals must be proficient time managers to fulfill their role as the instructional leader in their building. Time and energy become critical factors for school administrators who are committed to promoting instructional and professional growth. They will have to be adept at using their time and resources wisely. Following are brief discussions and descriptions of several common time and energy stealers that plague schools, with recommended strategies and tips.

NEGATIVE NELLIES

Negativity is cannibalistic. The more you feed it, the bigger and the stronger it grows.—Bobby Darin

There are people who go through life with a negative attitude and poor outlook. Unfortunately, some of these individuals are a part of the teaching profession and are in classrooms today. In some instances, they are excellent instructors, but are difficult to work with as colleagues in the school setting. They very seldom have anything positive to say in or outside of the classroom. They may push students to acquire skills and concepts but see progress as an uphill climb with very small or no gains. Negative Nellies hold low or limited expectations for their students' prognosis for growth and academic success.

Negative Nellies tend to put a damper on everything they are associated with, whether it's a faculty meeting, school/system-level committee, school-related extracurricular activity, or implementing a new program or initiative. They usually are very opinionated and delight in sharing their views and negative thoughts to whomever will listen. School leaders often expend precious time and energy attempting to bring them on board to thwart the impact of their negative attitudes on students, staff, parents, and other stakeholders. Steps need to be taken to minimize the effect a negative staff member may have on their time, resources, energy, and school climate.

Individuals who are negative usually are very unhappy about who and where they are in life. They tend to derive significance for themselves by tearing down or criticizing the ideas of others to gain a sense of significance for themselves. They delight in pain, hurt, and frustration caused by their negative verbal attacks on colleagues, family members, friends, and associates. Other Negative Nellies use past unfulfilled experiences, unhappy childhoods, and disappointments to fuel their negativity. School leaders must stand firm and eliminate the impact of negative employees on their staff.

Truths

- You can't change a person's attitude or personality.
- A person must be willing and want to change their attitude or personality.
- You can only control one person—yourself.

Strategies

- Accept your inability to change a person's attitude or personality.
- Bring your concerns regarding their negativity to the individual's attention.
- Devise a plan outlining specific behavior expected in the classroom and other areas.
- State positive and realistic statements about past successful solutions with similar problems.
- Link the Professional Development Plan to overall evaluation and monitor periodically throughout the school year.
- Acknowledge and celebrate improvements and professional gains.
- Refer for further action if there is no evidence of improvement.

Recommendations

- Guard yourself from becoming hooked in a cycle of negativity.
- Maintain your integrity and do not alter plans to mollify negative individuals.
- Choose your battles.
- Use negative remarks as potential problems to overcome.
- Don't take negative comments personally.

COMPLAINERS

Those who make the worst use of their time are the first to complain of its shortness.—Jean De La Bruyere

You are trying to complete a report in your office when you are interrupted by Teacher B: "Are you busy? May I come in for a minute?" You look up from your report and you want to reply, "No, I'm not busy. I'm sitting here doodling!" Before you can reply, however, Teacher B pulls up a chair and plops down next to your desk. This session is going to be longer than a minute. Teacher B has already bent your ear this morning complaining about the noise in the cafeteria, disrespectful parents in the car rider line, and the length of faculty meetings. Not a day goes by without Teacher B complaining and bringing something to your attention.

    School leaders have to listen with an open and objective mind. Occasionally, some of the complaints or issues brought to their attention are viable and legitimate. Legitimate complaints from staff should be addressed and handled as soon as possible. Everyday complainers usually whine continuously and consistently while implying that *you* need to do something about it. Their style of complaining can put school leaders on the defensive and lead to no-win situations or arguments. Administrators are also targeted by complainers and must avoid being drawn into an inescapable trap. It is hard to listen to complaints about your performance and control your emotions.

Chronic complainers perceive or view themselves as powerless, prescriptive, and perfect. They think they possess all solutions to how things should be done correctly. Additionally, they feel powerless to do anything about situations and want to appear blameless to peers and colleagues. Complaining gives them a false sense of superiority and perfection. Also, understanding the driving force behind chronic complainers' behavior is a critical factor. Interventions and strategies practiced by school administrators can lessen and thwart their attacks.

Truths

- Complainers find fault with everything and everyone.
- Complainers focus attention on themselves to get things done.
- There is usually some substance to their complaint(s).
- They place the responsibility for difficulties on others.
- Complainers seek sympathy and emotional validation.
- Complainers seek advice and solutions.

Strategies

- Grant a listening ear to the complaint(s).
- Convert the complaint into a solution conversation.
- Deflect the complaint and change the conversation, if possible.
- Listen attentively. The person may just want to vent.
- Address valid issues or complaints that are within your realm of responsibility.
- Don't agree with their complaint(s).
- Require complaint(s) be submitted in writing.

Recommendations

- Acknowledge the chronic complainer and note their concern.
- Make the chronic complainer feel heard.
- Avoid trying to convince the complainer that things aren't as they seem.
- Control the conversation and remain in control of your emotions.
- Avoid being defensive and apologetic.
- Move complainer into a problem-solving mode as soon as possible.

KNOW-IT-ALL EXPERTS

The dumbest people I know are those who know it all.—Malcolm Forbes

Every school leader's dream is to have a faculty of competent and effective teachers in every classroom. It may not be a realistic expectation, but certainly ensuring all students receive the best instruction possible is a worthy goal to strive toward. Most schools have teachers possessing, talents, gifts, and diverse levels of expertise. There are individuals who consider themselves experts in certain content or areas of curriculum. They aren't willing to open themselves to other ideas from colleagues or associates. They rely totally on their own successes and past experiences to support and maintain their know-it-all attitude and demeanor.

Know-it-all experts believe in their own superiority and can make those who have encounters with them feel humiliated, frustrated, angry, unintelligent, and powerless. They are argumentative and often respond to administrators, colleagues, and associates in a condescending manner. In staff meetings, they tend to dominate discussions and are very critical of others' recommendations or suggestions. What is frustrating and trying about the know-it-all is the fact that they have a good track record for being correct. This fact alone continuously feeds their superior attitude and strengthens their belief that they have the correct solution to issues or concerns. How do you handle these experts on your staff?

Truths

- Know-it-alls exude a powerful sense of superiority and personal authority.
- Know-it-alls have very little time or patience for the ideas and judgments of others.
- They are highly productive individuals with very little need for others.
- They see mistakes or problems as the fault of incompetents, not themselves.
- It is hard for them to accept or see errors in any project or plan they implement.

Strategies

- Listen attentively and acknowledge what is said to convey you understand what they are saying.
- Do your homework and gather your facts before presenting before know-it-alls.
- Paraphrase back to them the main points of their plan, idea being shared, or argument.

- Question and suggest, but don't confront know-it-alls.
- Ask questions firmly and offer alternatives for their consideration.

Recommendations

- Use a question format to present problems as additional information to be considered.
- Present alternatives as *what-ifs* to gain their attention and garner support.
- Guard yourself from becoming a know-it-all because of your professional experiences and skills.
- Use the knowledge and skills of the know-it-alls.
- Be open to and accepting of current techniques, information, and strategies when presented.

STROKE JUNKIES

Don't worry when you are not recognized, but strive to be worthy of recognition.—Abraham Lincoln

What causes effective classroom teachers to not believe and trust their capabilities as instructors? School leaders find this type of person not only a mystery, but also an unnecessary time stealer. These individuals must be told they are doing an excellent job or receive a pat on the back regardless of the assigned responsibility or task. Instead of being a valuable resource and peer leader for a staff, stroke junkies demand constant attention and confirmation from school administrators, colleagues, and associates. The need for constant approval often impedes their professional growth and personal development. They depend on and look to others for validation.

Sometime during their early childhood, these outwardly capable individuals, who crave constant approval, learned that they need to always look to others outside of themselves to feel productive and worthy. Being able to self-assess and determine next steps without the blessing of their parents, significant others, or peers is foreign to them. They lack confidence and initiative, despite being more than skilled and qualified. Moving forward and venturing into new territories is done hesitantly with reservation or trepidation if their move or idea isn't affirmed. Additionally, these individuals may be suffering from the desire to be perfect. They may have difficulty handling mistakes or imperfections.

Truths

- You will never be able to satisfy stroke junkies.
- Increasing recognition and approval only adds to their need for validation.

- There is a strong need to be liked and accepted.

Strategies

- Convey to staff that additional responsibilities are assigned based on skills, strengths, or capabilities.
- Acknowledge initiatives, steps, or projects implemented without your validation.
- Encourage staff willingness and attempt to move forward based on self-assessment.

Recommendations

- Ensure there are appropriate recognition strategies in place for all staff.
- Develop a staff recognition plan to address unique needs of school clientele.

NONPERFORMERS

> *Your assets are your employees. Invest more on those performing well. Let the non-performers go.*—Manoj Arora

All school administrators have had individuals on their staff who need additional support to enhance their instructional effectiveness in classrooms. A major responsibility of administrators as instructional leaders is ensuring students receive appropriate instruction for academic growth and skill development. We expect to spend additional time and resources to provide whatever is needed to enable professional growth and strengthen instructional delivery of individuals having difficulty as classroom instructors. School administrators use peer teachers, central office staff, instructional lead teachers, and academic coaches as resources during the improvement or remediation process.

Staff receives feedback on their classroom instructional performance as needed throughout the school year. The expectation is that with appropriate supplemental instructional support and resources, low-performing teachers' instructional effectiveness will be remediated and enhanced. There are individuals who occasionally do not put forth any effort to improve their performance. They focus on just doing enough to *get by* in the classroom. They have no interest or desire to improve their instructional prowess. It is these individuals who drain school administrators' limited time and energy. School leaders must take whatever steps are required to remove individuals who are not capable of improving.

There is a myriad of reasons why some individuals may not want to improve. Some staff members may have low self-esteem and may be unable to acquire skills needed to perform better in the classroom. Or they do little as possible to maintain their position without being released from their job. Others may shy away from implementing new instructional practices and programs with fidelity. Regardless of the underlying reasons offered for not wanting to improve or become more effective instructors, school leaders must focus on the most important clients in their building: students. Immediate action needs to be taken after attempts to remediate low-performing staff are unsuccessful.

Truths

- A person must want to become more effective.
- There are some people who are satisfied with status quo.
- You can't help everyone.

Strategies

- Develop a plan of action to address specific skill needs.
- Set a realistic time frame for improvement/growth.
- Supervise, monitor, and provide formative feedback.

Recommendations

- Enlist the help of other appropriate personnel to improve instructional performance.
- Plan professional development activities that focus on specific skill needs of staff.
- Involve the staff member in designing his or her professional improvement plan to promote buy-in.
- Celebrate and recognize improvements.

DRAMA KINGS AND QUEENS

Never let somebody's drama determine the outcome of your day.—Terry Mark

Many school leaders have had the opportunity during their career to face individuals who manage to have daily crises in their lives. If they aren't directly facing an alleged crisis, someone in their family or a close associate is in the throes of a crisis. They seem to thrive on running frantically from one situation to another and garnering as much attention as possible from others. Additionally, being the person called on as the *fixer* or *solution finder* satisfies a desire to be perceived as a leader among their peers. In several instances, these crises are minimal in nature and really aren't emergencies warranting immediate attention or resolution. They trap well-meaning leaders and staff in their drama.

School leaders must guard themselves and staff against the effect of drama kings and queens on school climate, culture, and school morale. Dramatic staff members often cause negative situations through gossip, lies, misrepresentations, and exaggerations. Their sense of high drama and need for attention can hamper school initiatives, professional learning activities, new program implementation, and classroom practices. School leaders may find their time and energy monopolized by responding to lengthy emails, putting out constant fires, and resolving personnel issues. The challenge for school leaders is remaining calm and focused.

Truths

- Drama kings and queens love an audience and participants.
- Drama kings and queens will create stormy situations for attention.
- Accept your inability to satisfy their need for drama and attention.
- Dramatic individuals feed off reactions received.

Strategies

- Distinguish real crises from manufactured crises.
- Set boundaries and specific guidelines for availability.
- Look at situations objectively.
- Gather all pertinent information concerning a situation before acting.
- Remain calm and in control of your reactions.
- Limit attention given to inappropriate behavior or outbursts.

Recommendations

- Don't allow yourself to be drawn into drama.
- Choose how you respond to situations and dramatic individuals.
- Reward and acknowledge composure, not chaotic behavior.
- Refrain from engaging in conversations until there's evidence of emotional control.

CHRONIC ALMOST-LINE-CROSSERS

If you're going to do something tonight that you'll be sorry for tomorrow morning, sleep late.—Henny Youngman

You have just completed a conference with a staff member who you had spoken to previously about a specific matter. This isn't the first time you've had to address this issue with the teacher. As a matter of fact, you felt this incident would not occur again. The teacher assured you that she understood your expectation for future handlings of the situation. Well, it's happened again, and now you must schedule another conference with the teacher and write a follow-up memo. Why couldn't the infraction be a major one? Have you spent an enormous amount of time and energy on a person who continuously steps to the line, but not over it?

What causes this predictable behavior? Are they risk takers or simply determined to go as far as possible without reaching the limit? There are individuals, however, who derive pleasure from making life difficult and unpleasant for their family and associates. They usually know their rights as professional educators like the back of their hand. The driving force behind any action for them seems to be control. If they gain control of the situation, school leaders may lose their objectivity and school focus. The misuse of these calculating individuals' talents and skills is a detriment to principals, staff, and schools.

Truths

- There are individuals with ulterior motives.
- Your style of leadership is not accepted unequivocally by all.

Strategies

- Control and guard your reactions and actions.
- Identify and know your *buttons*.
- Develop a realistic and reasonable improvement plan.
- Supervise, monitor, and document.

Recommendations

- Act immediately if a directive is disobeyed.
- Set strong consequences to discourage repeated inappropriate behavior.
- Communicate (orally) with a witness present.
- Respond to questions formally (written).
- Acknowledge and celebrate adherence to rules/directives and improvements.

GOSSIP CARRIERS AND BAD NEWS BEARERS

Great minds discuss ideas. Average minds discuss events. Small minds discuss people.—Henry Thomas Buckle

Do you have a staff member who greets you daily with something they have either heard or were told by a very reliable source who is "in the know"? Of course, it is usually negative and spreads like wildfire. You are bombarded with emails from school personnel and occasionally parents because somehow the rumor or gossip has made its way into the community. These gossip carriers pride themselves on being in the know and often have their own supporters who look to them for the latest gossip or juicy news. School administrators are usually unaware of negative gossip until it's brought to their office as a situation to resolve.

Does this sound familiar? As school leaders, we often spend time resolving situations among students and parents. We don't anticipate or expect to expend valuable time tracking down the gossip source, soothing hurt feelings, or trying to restore working relationships. There are some individuals who enjoy causing unnecessary problems by spreading gossip or rumors about their colleagues or associates. They thrive on confusion, drama, and turmoil brought about by their actions. Gossipers enjoy being in the spotlight momentarily, even if it is negative. Their desire for attention overrides supporting and encouraging colleagues. Individuals who spread negativity are unhappy and hurting themselves.

Truths

- People love to hear gossip about their friends and enemies.
- Individuals may forgive, but don't forget hurtful things said about them.

Strategies

- Control your reaction to negative news or gossip.
- Require the source and documented facts.
- Request a written statement and signature.

Recommendations

- Refrain from discussing personal matters with school personnel.
- Do not repeat or share anything that has not been confirmed as true or accurate.

Chapter 3

POOR COMMUNICATORS

The single biggest problem in communication is the illusion that it has taken place.—George Bernard Shaw

Communication. Communication. Communication. For school leaders, teachers, and other school clientele, communication is a key ingredient needed to operate and maintain high-functioning schools. All school leaders' responsibilities and administrative tasks are tied to communication. The lack of effective communication can harm and cause irreparable damage to schools. Individuals who are ineffective communicators thwart professional growth, progress, academic achievement, and goal obtainment. Their inability to communicate honestly and sincerely with parents impacts a leader's time and energy.

Most school leaders have experienced having a teacher or staff member who manages to relay inappropriate information or cause hurt feelings when meeting with parents or other stakeholders. An administrator relies on his or her staff being able to communicate effectively with their students, parents, and stakeholders. Upset parents and stakeholders usually contact school administrators or appropriate central office personnel to report their displeasure. As a result, principals find themselves scheduling a meeting with the teacher or staff member to confirm or deny the report. In some instances, several meetings are required for a resolution.

Truths

- There are poor communicators.
- Communication can be improved.
- Some people are unwilling to accept their inability to communicate effectively.

Strategies

- Provide communication professional learning periodically.
- Assign appropriate personnel to guide and monitor conferences.
- Require written summaries of conferences with specific outcomes indicated.

Recommendations

- Schedule and plan annual evaluations to assess communication effectiveness.
- Keep abreast of techniques and strategies to improve communication.

PASSIVE-AGGRESSIVE PEOPLE

Passive-aggressive behavior consumes unnecessary time and resources. Say what you mean, let's resolve the issue, and move on to more productive tasks.
—Izey Victoria Odiase

You have just finished a conference with a staff member and feel nothing has been resolved or accomplished. You know that you will probably have to meet with this individual again soon about another matter. No matter what you say, recommend, or suggest, it's received with a pleasant smile and silent acquiescence. Beneath the surface of that smile lies hostility and aggression. It is never displayed openly or expressed directly. Passive-aggressive individuals never show their hand and continue to repeat passive-aggressive behaviors over time. Dealing with a passive-aggressive person is frustrating and uncomfortable.

What causes individuals to develop into passive-aggressive people? Is it the result of early childhood trauma, inappropriate parenting, or negative life experiences? Reasons why a person may resort to passive-aggressive behaviors are very complex and deep-rooted. Principals, however, may experience behaviors such as silent treatment, avoidance, stonewalling, anger, backstabbing, negative comments, defensiveness, blaming, and resistance. These behaviors alone make it very difficult to work and reason rationally to resolve issues or clarify misunderstandings. Colleagues and associates limit their involvement and interaction with their passive-aggressive peers in the building.

Truths

- Passive-aggressive individuals don't accept their responsibility in situations.
- You cannot win an argument or have a rational discussion with a passive-aggressive person.
- Tolerating a passive-aggressive individual encourages and intensifies their behaviors.

Strategies

- Control your behavior and actions.
- Take charge of your attitude, and don't personalize inappropriate comments.
- Avoid being drawn into unnecessary arguments.
- Offer strong consequences for inappropriate behaviors.
- Use humor to defuse a situation/interaction, if it's a mild incident.

Recommendations

- Display composure when confronted by a passive-aggressive person.
- Communicate formally (written) with a passive-aggressive person.
- Have a third party (witness) present during conferences/conversations.
- Record facts and investigate incidents or allegations thoroughly.

ME NOT WE

Unity is strength. . . . When there is teamwork and collaboration, wonderful things can be achieved.—Mattie Stepanek

All principals know the importance teamwork plays among staff in schools. When teaching positions and other key openings occur in schools, school administrators make a concerted effort to fill slots with not only capable prospective staff members, but also individuals who will be able to work with their grade-level team members and peer colleagues collaboratively. School leaders may have a teacher or staff member who prefers working alone rather than plan with others. These individuals attend grade-level planning or staff meetings and lead team members to think they're on board with all final decisions decided upon.

School administrators are committed to developing and fostering a work environment that consists of teamwork and collaboration. Teachers and staff who work together collectively promote professional growth and obtainment of school goals. Individuals who seem to have their own agendas or ideas can impede the efforts of their grade-level team members by displaying an unwillingness to work toward established school goals and initiatives. Why are some individuals against team collaboration? Reasons for a lack of cooperation and collaboration are varied. Individuals have difficulty socializing, sharing ideas, and relying on the knowledge of others.

Surprisingly, many non–team players are out-of-the-box thinkers with creative solutions and thought-provoking ideas that help staff and schools grow. Others may not understand the expectation of their role as a member of a team, or past experiences with working on teams has led them to not trust and rely on others to do their part of a task. School leaders address the non-teamwork behaviors because of complaints from frustrated grade-level team members. For principals, the task becomes effectively communicating the importance of teamwork and finding the best means for harnessing and utilizing skills and talents of non–team players in their building.

Truths

- Everyone is not a people person.

- There are people who work better alone.

Strategies

- Clearly state and communicate your expectations for teamwork.
- Involve the team members in resolving their team collaboration issues.
- Meet with non–team players to determine why they aren't interested in working as a team.
- Provide appropriate resources, professional learning, and training on collaboration.
- Develop specific guidelines for the grade-level teams.
- Consider the strengths of the non–team player and determine if there is a more suitable role as a member of the grade-level team.

Recommendations

- Address teamwork issues that may arise immediately.
- Model teamwork and collaboration as the school leader.
- Promote, publicize, and celebrate completed projects and activities involving teamwork.
- If a team member's uncooperative behavior is disruptive, seek further disciplinary action.

HEALTH-HAZARD, TOXIC PEOPLE

Toxic people attach themselves like cinder blocks tied to your ankles and then invite you for a swim in their poisoned waters.—John Mark Green

Toxic people walk around with perpetual storm clouds over their heads. They are continually wrestling with one issue or another. Toxic people may disguise themselves as friends, family members, and yes, even teachers. These individuals are usually manipulative and know how to use drama to draw others into their circle of misery. Administrators must guard and protect themselves from the grasp of toxic staff members. Key to avoiding entrapment is recognizing a toxic individual and knowing how to handle them appropriately.

The best way to recognize a toxic person is assessing how you feel when interacting with them. Encounters with toxic individuals are emotionally draining, exhausting, and negative. They always have problems and are experts at manipulating situations and feelings. Additionally, these toxic staff members are unsupportive, verbally abusive, judgmental, needy, and highly critical of school leaders and colleagues. They don't take responsibility for any of their actions or behaviors. School leaders may be targeted and considered responsible for a toxic staff member's problem. They perceive school administrators' main responsibility to be *fixing* their problems.

Following are warning signs of possible entrapment by a toxic staff member:

- You are placed in and always made responsible for situations they have caused.
- Your attention and time are constantly demanded by the toxic individual.
- You watch what you say around them to avoid or discourage emotional outbursts.
- You dread any form of contact or communication with the toxic staff member.
- Your workday is consistently monopolized by handling the toxic individuals' concerns and issues.

Truth

- You cannot change the mind-set of a toxic individual.

Strategies

- Limit daily direct contact with the individual.
- Set specific guidelines and parameters for communication and behavior.
- Refrain from meeting with the toxic staff member alone.
- Use written communication.

CHAPTER 3 SUMMARY

As instructional leaders, school administrators are charged with the responsibility of supervising staff under their leadership. They are expected to monitor classroom instruction, provide professional learning opportunities, and encourage continued professional growth of staff and other pertinent school clientele. Meeting the needs of teachers and other school clientele is a daunting but rewarding task. To meet this challenge, school leaders must become effective time managers and guardians of their time and energy. The focus of this chapter was on problem personnel that potentially lessen school administrators' impact on staff professional growth.

The author discussed selected staff behaviors that are common to most schools. There may be, however, other problem personnel not represented. A principal's role as an instructional leader is paramount to guaranteeing continuous staff growth, academic achievement, and professional development. The truths, strategies, and recommendations shared serve as guidelines for neutralizing and minimizing the detrimental effects of problem personnel.

School administrators must become better managers of their time and energy to address staff needs effectively and efficiently.

GOING DEEPER

Time to Reflect

1. Are you currently experiencing a personnel issue that is consuming your time and energy?
2. What strategy(ies) have you implemented to maximize your time and energy?
3. List strategies and/or professional learning activities that have been very effective in improving classroom instructional practices and teaching skills.
4. Do you have access to additional resources (school or central office level) to help you address personnel issues? If not, what other sources of assistance are available outside your school system?
5. Informally survey your staff to assess strengths and areas needing further development.
6. Develop a plan utilizing staff strength to improve weak areas of selected teachers.
7. Contact a local university or college to explore services you may utilize with your staff.
8. Develop a list of recommended outside resource people skilled in areas or topics needed for professional growth opportunities.

Chapter Four

School Leaders Need Love Too

Coping with Criticism, Stress, and Anxiety

> *Love yourself enough to set boundaries. Your time and energy are precious. You get to choose how to use it. Teach people how to treat you by deciding what you will and won't accept.* —Anna Taylor

CRITICISM

School leaders of today face a variety of challenges as instructional leaders. They are expected to address federal and state mandates, respond to cries for accountability, guarantee growth and achievement for all students, and manage highly effective schools. In addition to supervising and monitoring the overall operation of the school, administrators have the daunting task of handling student discipline, responding to parent and staff concerns, and overseeing the facility. As change agents in their buildings, administrators endure unpleasant side effects of their highly visible position. They are targets of scrutiny, complaints, and negative comments.

Dealing with criticism and negativity is not an easy task for administrators. Once you become the instructional leader in a school, you must accept criticism, negative comments, and complaints as unpleasant aspects of your position. It is impossible to please everyone with decisions made to address student, parent, and staff concerns. School leaders who attempt to offer solutions or implement policies to satisfy everyone will compromise their basic beliefs and values. Leading schools is about always doing what is right for the organization. Being able to make tough decisions despite opposing views is the mark of an effective leader.

Although a variety of criticism or negative comments may be aimed at school leaders, the main reason why individuals criticize is because of their perception that something is not working for them or the school. When individuals feel powerless to initiate change and innovations, administrators become the target of their discontent. School leaders also need to accept the fact they aren't perfect and do make mistakes. There are ideas or actions recommended by staff that are more effective and innovative. Coping with criticism appropriately enhances a leader's overall effectiveness. Following are ways to address criticism in a positive manner:

- Don't become defensive or angry and make excuses. The criticism or negative comment is not directed at you personally. They are criticizing your work, not you. Who you are as a person isn't diminished by criticism or negative comments. School leaders must exercise caution to ensure they are not trying to justify their actions and decisions. Trying to justify decisions or actions may lead to comparing themselves to others and pointing out their failures. Bragging about past successes and projects places you in a defensive stance.
- Listen to the criticism and make sure you have a clear understanding of the comment. Ask questions about the criticism or negative comment for clarification. Manage and control your behavior and actions when receiving criticism.
- Serve as a role model for how you should conduct yourself when criticized. Let your teachers see good reactions to criticism and negative comments. Remember, you are a walking billboard for your staff, parents, and students. School clientele will learn it's okay to make errors and that you are willing to alter your tactics for a more effective way.
- Assume individuals criticizing have good intentions and are not *out to get you* unless it is proven otherwise. Reflect over the criticism. Examine the criticism or negative comment thoroughly to see if there is a credible truth in the criticism or negative comment. Looking for and pulling out positives will benefit you and the staff. Criticism or negative comments that are nasty and destructive should not be taken to heart. Feedback of this type should be ignored. Continue to move on. Focus on the feedback that moves you and your school forward.
- See criticism as help. Use the feedback received to improve what you are currently doing. Feedback received (positive and negative) is a sign that people are interested in and concerned about your job performance. Constructive feedback helps you develop and grow as a school leader. You don't want to create a school culture that fosters a climate discouraging other points of view or ideas. School leaders need to know when they are mistaken and should be open to receiving other perspectives.

- Everyone makes mistakes and needs to learn from them. Making mistakes doesn't thwart your leadership abilities and skills. School leaders do benefit from errors and wrong decisions. There are major problems if administrators continue making the same mistakes because they refuse to accept, acknowledge, and use constructive criticism to learn.
- Separate praise and blame from success and failure. Everyone loves to receive praise and recognition for projects and accomplishments. We have no difficulty accepting accolades. As leaders, we must be willing to accept criticism and accountability when things go wrong. Neither criticism nor praise determine a project's success. Also, praise your staff when a job is done well even if you don't agree. Never use praise to deflect possible criticism from staff or force conformity to your way of thinking.
- Acknowledge and accept criticism as a necessary evil. School leaders who are never criticized aren't focusing on the goals of their school. You can't be an effective leader trying to satisfy everyone's agenda. You need to develop a thick skin and mental toughness. Leadership is not a personality contest. If you are willing to face whatever comes in the wake of possible criticism for the good of the organization, you are well on the way to bringing about changes that promote growth.

STRESS

The constant bombardment of discipline problems, personnel issues, parent concerns, budgetary cutbacks, curriculum updates, and classroom instructional practices drains individuals. Continuous subjection to stressful situations or incidents has an impact on a person's job performance and overall well-being. School leaders' job-related responsibilities can cause chronic stress and result in burnout over time if not managed or handled appropriately. School leaders are subject to emotional and physiological damage by the mere function of their leadership role.

By the nature of their positions as school leaders, they naturally worry or think about effectiveness. Administrators are concerned about resolving issues, meeting needs of school clientele, and accomplishing school goals. Any of these may be sources of stress for school leaders. Stress, however, is an essential part of life in general and is controllable. What is important is how principals manage and control stress. Are school administrators able to protect themselves from the debilitating effects of excessive exposure to uncontrolled stress? Can they continue to serve as productive and effective change agents for schools?

Regardless of what we do or where we are, it is natural for us, as human beings, to worry and bring stress in our lives. There also are myths about stress that are held by many people.

They are:

- *Stress is the same for everybody.* This is not true. School leaders have different personalities and leadership styles. What might be a stressful situation or event for one leader may not be stressful for another school administrator.
- *Stress is always bad for you.* Stress can be negative or positive. The effects of stress can spur you on or thwart your growth. How leaders manage stress is the critical factor.
- *Stress is everywhere. There isn't anything you can do about stress.* This is not true. Something can be done about stress. School leaders can choose how to manage and cope with situations or challenges they encounter. Their perspective is key in coping with stress.
- *If there are no symptoms, there's no stress.* This is not true. Covering symptoms with medications or other supplements does not lessen the impact of stress on the body and an individual's job performance.
- *Only major symptoms of stress require attention.* School leaders need to address any symptom of stress they may be experiencing such as headaches, backaches, insomnia, and heartburn. No symptoms need to be ignored. Stress symptoms signal that things are off track or getting out of hand. Stress and worry are a part of life, but school leaders should ensure that stress doesn't keep them from enjoying life and being productive in their work.

How are school leaders guarding and revitalizing themselves to withstand and cope with ongoing challenges and changes encountered throughout the school year? What strategies and techniques are used by school leaders to help them stay the course and maintain their focus regardless of situations, changes, and initiatives they are required to address or achieve?

Veteran and new school leaders use a variety of resources and strategies to help them cope with the stresses and responsibilities of their job. They expend an enormous amount of time looking after everyone else's welfare except their own. School clientele generally do not perceive their school leaders as needing emotional care and support. They are more likely to question or criticize than support building-level leaders. Their focus is centered on what they need and not the entire school. A school leader focuses on overall schoolwide needs. The different focuses cause frustrations and discontentment among school clientele and school leaders.

ANXIETY

All administrators strive to be effective and successful. Their work environments and experiences can lead leaders to be anxious about their job performance. School leaders and people in general are less anxious when things go the way they want without difficulty. However, when desires, goals, and wants are blocked or thwarted, leaders can become paralyzed with anxiety and fearfulness. Once anxiety has a foothold in their life, creativity and self-confidence erode slowly. They are no longer able to focus on school goals and initiatives without worrying about or fearing failure or criticism.

They begin to question their ability to make sound decisions or become careless, missing significant signs or implications. Once anxiety gains a foothold in the daily operation of a leader, things unravel quickly. Staff notice the principal's hesitancy and increase the school leader's anxiety through their lack of support. A vicious cycle ensues, limiting the professional growth of school leaders and their teachers.

Administrators often set high, unrealistic expectations on themselves and let *must-haves* rule their very existence. They must have perfect test scores and complete support and buy-in from every staff member, and never have any personnel problems or suffer any adversity. Demands and pressures from federal and state mandates add anxiety to an already ever-challenging role for school administrators. Although anxiety does have negative effects on a person's performance, it can also be healthy. Anxiety, if used in a healthy context, does help ward off danger by making you aware of things that may be harmful. Principals must control anxiety.

HEALTHY AND UNHEALTHY ANXIETY

Healthy anxiety is life preserving and is characterized by being cautious and generally leads to satisfactory results. School leaders with healthy anxiety are in control of their feelings and emotions. They make sound decisions and cope with difficult circumstances or situations in an efficient manner. Administrators who are overly anxious and suffer from unhealthy anxiety have panic attacks and are unable to cope with tough situations or predicaments. Unhealthy anxiety takes the form of terror, phobias, panic attacks, numbness, and other physical ailments. Healthy anxiety involves caution and vigilance, which ward off potential harm.

An unhealthy obsessive focus on anxiety, however, also thwarts creative thinking and limits problem solving. School leaders who are overly anxious about their job and performance perform poorly and develop unrealistic expectations for themselves and their work environment. Because of their unrealistic expectations and misguided perceptions, overly anxious school leaders prevent their staff from trying different initiatives for fear of failure and ineffectiveness. As a result, they become poor agents of change and are unable to lead their school toward continuous growth and school improvement.

One major fact school leaders must accept is that events, situations, demands, federal and state mandates, and curriculum changes do not cause anxiety. How leaders handle or think about what transpires on their jobs day to day is key to overcoming the negative impact of anxiety. When their *must-haves* don't become realities, school administrators become panic ridden and may suffer from depression. Losing their self-confidence, school leaders begin to question their leadership capabilities and may doubt decisions and ideas. Administrators can minimize and control unhealthy anxiety by implementing and utilizing proactive actions.

Following is a brief discussion of strategies, techniques, and resources school leaders use to minimize the effect of energy and time stealers in schools. By utilizing these recommended school-level strategies and resources, school leaders have been able to stay the course and withstand the stress of their jobs. They have been able to lead effective schools, serve as positive role models, and protect their physical and emotional well-being.

- *Teacher Leaders/Grade-Level Chairpersons*: Individuals assigned to these positions have demonstrated content strength and leadership skills. They are well respected by their peers and colleagues. School leaders utilize them to mentor and train other teachers, model lessons, and assist with monitoring classroom instruction and practices.
- *Assistant Principals/Instructional Lead Teachers*: Individuals in this position are certified to assist the school leader with staff evaluations and the overall operation of the building. They also have experience with curriculum and can provide professional growth activities, if needed.
- *Leadership Team*: This team usually consists of representatives from each grade level and other key positions in the building such as a media specialist, school counselor, office manager, paraprofessional, custodian, and cafeteria manager. A leadership team is an effective vehicle to communicate with all school clientele. It also provides the opportunity to share concerns or issues. Buy-in and support for schoolwide initiatives and decisions are encouraged and fostered through leadership team involvement.
- *Special Education Staff and Lead Teachers*: Special education teachers and special education lead teachers are a valuable school- and district-level human resource for school leaders. Their specialized training and knowledge assist regular education staff and parents in understanding Individualized Education Plans and other special education requirements for special-needs students.

- *Central Office–Level Administrators*: Many school systems have central office staff who keep abreast of curriculum updates, federal and state mandates, testing, initiatives, and classroom practices for selected content areas. They also serve as a resource and mentor for school leaders. School leaders call on them to assist with implementing innovative programs, writing grants, observing classrooms, conferencing with parents, and providing professional growth activities for staff.
- *State Departments of Education*: Every state has a department that oversees the education of all students in the state. Selected individuals with expertise in specific content areas are charged with the responsibility of keeping abreast of curriculum and innovative instructional practices. They develop and design curriculum needed to meet each state's standards. State departments of education also furnish training and updates when state- or federal-mandated changes are approved for implementation statewide.
- *Local Colleges and Universities*: Colleges and universities welcome the opportunity to partner with local school systems in their service area. Their teaching staff can serve as consultants for local schools and school systems. This mutual relationship between local schools and higher education institutions enables collaboration between school leaders and colleges or universities. School administrators and teachers are exposed to research and trends in education. Classrooms become learning laboratories for leaders and future teachers.
- *Regional Educational Service Agency*: Many states have established regional service areas supported by state funds whose primary purpose is to assist participating school systems located in selected areas or regions in professional learning, purchasing, school improvement, planning, curriculum instruction, specialized services such as audiology, and other needed services. These service agencies are staffed with individuals who have expertise in a variety of content areas and programs.

School leaders of participating school districts may schedule times for selected consultants to present workshops or train staff on innovative programs or the latest instructional classroom practices. School systems pay an annual fee to join regional educational service agencies that work in conjunction with state departments of education. Annual needs assessments are conducted to address school improvement needs or initiatives. School leaders may schedule technical assistance and professional learning for themselves or their school staff:

- *Professional Organizations*: There are several professional organizations such as the Association of Supervision and Curriculum Development (ASCD) and other similar professional organizations that keep school leaders abreast of current trends and issues concerning supervision, curriculum, and instruction. Many school administrators use their resources to strengthen their effectiveness as instructional leaders and change agents. Professional organizations also offer participating members tips, techniques, resources, and strategies that address and meet specific individual school and system needs.

The preceding list of resources isn't all inclusive. It is important for administrators to use all appropriate personnel and resources available to help ease the responsibility and lighten the heavy load of supervising teachers and monitoring the school's instructional programs. School leaders who underutilize people, resources, services, and assistance organizations limit the quantity and quality of assistance that staff receive to improve classroom performance and increase student achievement.

Getting through rough days and tough situations is a challenge for veteran and new school leaders. No matter how long administrators have a school, they employ a variety of strategies and techniques to revitalize themselves to face and handle whatever changes or situations may come their way. Several school leaders shared and recommended tips that personally worked for them. These selected techniques kept them positive, centered, and focused on why they became leaders—love for students. As one administrator said, "I think about the children. They matter. Focusing on the students kept me returning everyday ready to touch a child in a positive way."

SCHOOL LEADERS' PERSONAL TIPS, STRATEGIES, AND TECHNIQUES

- *Sounding Boards*: Find someone you can trust to air your feelings or simply get things off your chest. School administrators use their spouse, close friends, mentors, or peer colleagues as sounding boards. Individuals employed outside school systems can be sounding boards. Sometimes people who work outside the school system are more objective and present a unique perspective on the incident or situation.
- *Meditating*: Spend time reflecting on scriptures or positive affirmation statements to remain hopeful and positive. Many school leaders set aside time early in the morning or in the evening as quiet thinking time. Some leaders post scripture and affirmations in their office as reminders throughout the day. A popular affirmation used among school leaders is "This too shall pass."
- *Journaling*: Setting aside time during the day to reflect and write about what happened is a way to relieve stress and anxiety. Writing allows you to express on paper your inner thoughts and feelings. This process not

only is soothing and calming but also provides time for brainstorming viable solutions.
- *Positive Affirmations*: Engaging in positive self-talk not only reduces anxiety and stress in lives but also cures ills from negativity and criticism. School leaders should develop an unobstructed vision of their goals and a viable plan for accomplishing them. Consider barriers or obstacles to goals and enlist your cheerleaders, positive affirmations, to lead the way. Positive affirmations should be visible and spoken out loud throughout the day. Positive affirmations are effective when they are clear and short, stated in positive terms, written about yourself, kept in handy places, and recorded during pleasant moods.
- Following are suggested examples of effective positive affirmations for school leaders to utilize, if applicable:

    1. My body, mind, and spirit are joyful, happy, and energized.
    2. There is a solution for every obstacle I may encounter.
    3. I see humor in myself and situations.
    4. I embrace myself with love and self-worth.
    5. I am worthy.
    6. I will be in the present each day.
    7. I am delighting in the moment.
    8. I care for myself.
    9. I am capable and creative.
    10. I will survive.
    11. I am grateful and thankful.
    12. Deadlines won't destroy me.
    13. I will persevere.
    14. I support myself with loving family and friends.
    15. I learn from mistakes.
    16. I am human, not perfect.
    17. I will laugh and smile daily.
    18. Tomorrow is another day.
    19. I determine my destiny.
    20. I trust and believe in myself.

- *Changing the Scenery or Setting*: There are times when being in the area or room where the encounter or situation took place causes anxiety. Simply removing yourself from the area or room relieves tension and negativity. Some school leaders have suggested that walking the halls, visiting classrooms, eating lunch with students, or visiting the playground helped them refocus on their main purpose. Contact with students eased feelings of frustration, anxiety, or anger.

- *Exercising*: Physical activity such as walking, swimming, working out, and bowling helps the body counteract the effects of stress and emotional lows. Some school leaders reported that having planned physical activities not only reenergized them but also promoted feelings of well-being and positivity.
- *Praying*: A consistent prayer life can enable school leaders to use their faith and spiritual beliefs to serve as anchors when confronted with undue pressure and unpleasant situations. They can also pray before the beginning of each workday to remain centered and focused on their purpose.
- *Sense of Humor*: Having a sense of humor is an important quality to possess to manage and cope with negativity and criticism. It may be difficult to find the humor in a situation while it is occurring. However, if you're able to reflect later and joke about it, you'll ease some of the tension and be in a better frame of mind. Humor and laughter positively affect the body by helping you breathe deeper, lowering blood pressure and pulse, and contracting muscles. Laughter relaxes the body, boosts the immune system, and reduces the production of cortisol—the stress hormone.
- *Listening to Music*: Music is well known for its therapeutic value. There are proven benefits attributed to listening to music and its effect on the body. Researchers claim dopamine is released in the brain while listening to music, which promotes a feeling of well-being. Music releases stress and is utilized by school administrators to place themselves in a calm and soothing work environment. Sitting quietly and listening to music revitalizes the body, changes moods, and refreshes the mind.
- *Mentors*: Experienced colleagues and peers make excellent mentors for veteran and new leaders. They serve as sounding boards and role models. Their prior experiences, knowledge, and skills serve as guideposts for school leaders who are seeking different perspectives or new insights about managing a personnel matter.
- *Positive Thinking*: Keeping positive thoughts is easier to say than do. School leaders do have days when they feel overwhelmed with discipline problems, parent complaints, and personnel problems. Negative thoughts, like negative comments, can affect a person's attitude and mood. It is important to dispel negative and unhealthy thoughts before you become fixated on them. Thinking about the worst thing that could happen and noting that it didn't happen helps administrators gain a better appreciation for what they did do successfully. School administrators must strive to eliminate negative thoughts.
- *"I Am Grateful" Notebook*: An effortless way to obtain a positive outlook on life regardless of what is going on around you is to acknowledge daily things you are grateful for. A small notebook or tablet and pencil by your

bedside is the perfect way to jot down your thoughts early in the morning. Review your musings later in the day or early evening.
- *Stress Diary*: Note situations that are stressful or that cause stress. Note the date, time, and situation. Jot down who was present during the episode or situation. Try to determine the triggers for your stress. Devise a plan to lessen the stress associated with the situation or activity. Find interventions to minimize or relieve your stress and monitor your progress.
- *Relaxation Techniques*: Compile a list or collection of simple, easy-to-do activities to help your body relax. For example, focusing on selected positive words or phrases helps the body relax. Search the internet for exercises that may be performed in an office.
- *Success and Accomplishment Log*: Facing challenges and resolving issues and dealing with discipline problems daily can drain the life of school administrators. It is easy to focus on what went wrong in the run of a day and not keep up with the success. It is recommended to log the successes and accomplishments. Reflecting on things that were resolved without difficulty helps principals maintain a positive perspective and outlook.
- *Praise or Warm, Fuzzy File*: Keeping a collection of cards, positive notes, and letters from staff, parents, students, and other clientele to perk you up during down times is an effective to lift spirits when you are feeling unappreciated. Rereading these notes will be a nice reminder of the days and times people were satisfied and pleased with what you accomplished for them. It is also a reminder that you will have more days like the previous days soon.
- *Make Time to Laugh*: One school leader reported that keeping a daily *Far Side* calendar on her desk provided something to laugh about every day to relieve stress. Listening to jokes and finding funny cartoons will keep your office full of laughter. These cartoons and jokes may be shared with other colleagues and associates.
- *Surf the Net*: Setting aside to relieve stress by searching the internet for different certificates, great lesson plans, school activities, or school graphics is another way to relieve anxiety and tenseness. Additionally, surfing the net enables school leaders to do something constructive and helpful while easing their minds and relaxing.
- *Spend Time with Students*: Several administrators suggest leaving the office and walking around the building visiting students to release tension and alleviate stress. Make it a point to start and end each day on a positive note. Go where the children are and engage them in meaningful conversations about their day. Volunteer to read to a class. Classroom teachers and students enjoy this special treat.
- *Expanding Your Horizon*: School administrators recommended doing other education-related activities like writing articles, teaching a class, or serving as a presenter to relieve stress, increase confidence, and open other

opportunities for growth and intellectual development. Sharing your experiences and knowledge with others increases your knowledge and skill base.
- *Read*: Reading books of your own choosing is offered as an excellent technique to relieve the mind of the day's worries. One school administrator who loves mysteries reads every night to shut off events of the day to get a good night's rest.
- *Enjoy Nature*: Another principal walks outside when things become stressful for her during the day. Walks through local parks or neighborhoods clear thinking as you walk and observe nature. Also, the sun has a therapeutic effect on the body and is a free mood enhancer. Sunlight makes people feel better and increases the level of serotonin in the brain, which improves mood. A brief stroll outside around your building will lift spirits and brighten hectic, stressful workdays.
- *Don't Take Stress Home*: This simple recommendation is probably hard to do. All school leaders struggle with not taking stress as well as work home. Once this task is accomplished, life at home will be more relaxing and stress free. Being able to spend a restful evening at home enables leaders to return to work with a fresh start and renewed mind daily.
- *Spend Time with Pets*: Several animal-loving administrators stated that quality time spent with their pets was key in helping them ease tensions and the effect of stress. Caring for their pets took their minds off the issues and problems of the day.
- *Quality Time with Friends*: Plan activities, get-togethers, or special trips with close friends or associates. Give yourself something to look forward to during the week in addition to your job. Enjoy moments and leave the mishaps of the workday behind. Replace anxiety and work with joy and excitement. Revitalize your thoughts and day with positive activities.
- *Work in the Garden*: There is something about feeling dirt between your fingers, planting seeds, and smelling the aroma of flowers in a garden that soothes the soul and lightens the heart. If you don't have a garden, a principal highly recommends starting one. He sees the opportunity to work outside in his yard or garden as relaxing and fulfilling.
- *Planning and Managing Time*: According to two school leaders, planning and managing their time well eliminates a lot of stress. If time is taken to plan, you have a better chance to think through situations and assess what can possibly happen or go wrong. They also stated that managing their time enables them to stay ahead of their work or catch up. This prevents them from crashing and burning out.
- *Work-at-Home Day*: Another school leader manages his time and relieves the effect of stress by planning a *work-at-home day* pending school board approval. His greatest source of stress is work overload from his job—too much to do with too little time. He found periodically working uninter-

rupted at home not only helped him catch up but also greatly released stress and worry about unfinished reports and tasks. Being at home, he was able to work without phone calls, meetings, and other unexpected interruptions. He felt a sense of accomplishment just being able to finish several tasks. Although he was still doing schoolwork, he felt fulfilled.

- *Take a Fun Class*: Several administrators advised taking a fun class of your choosing. Rediscover a past hobby or learn a new skill. Weekend and evening classes such as painting, jewelry making, crocheting, knitting, woodworking, ceramics, and sewing unlock creativity and use other skills and abilities that may have been dormant or untapped for years. Share your experiences with colleagues and associates. Let your staff see another side of you.
- *Heal and Nurture Yourself*: Principals must be responsible for healing and supporting themselves. They need to take time to listen to themselves and their body. Administrators should treat themselves to fun and pleasure and be their own cheerleader. Also, they can heal themselves by touching someone else's life, believe in their own self-worth, and see challenges as opportunities and not failures.
- *Take the Weekend Off*: Many school leaders spend weekends working on school stuff to catch up or stay ahead. By doing so, they have no break from their job. Before they know it, the weekend is over and they're back in their office early Monday morning. To allow a nice break and rest from stress, many administrators take weekends off from work and plan fun activities, not work, for the weekend. Use weekends to reconnect with family, former colleagues, and old friends.
- *Time Out in a Vacant Classroom*: Another recommended strategy to use when overcome with stress during the day is to find an empty classroom. One principal shared how she sought an empty classroom for peace and quiet time for thirty minutes. Sitting in the quiet, dark classroom gave her the opportunity to destress and relax. Once thirty minutes passed, she returned to her office in a better frame of mind ready to tackle the remainder of the day.
- *Take the Spotlight off Yourself*: Thinking about and helping others is a way to minimize focusing on yourself. Reaching out to someone in need or being a Big Brother or Big Sister to a middle or high school student not only is rewarding but also helps you feel better. This is an excellent way to relieve tension, worry, and anxiety.
- *Singing in the Shower*: You may not be able to carry a tune or think you have the worst voice in the world, but nothing lifts the spirits or soothes the mind more than singing. Release your inhibitions and stress through songs while showering or bathing.
- *Garbage In and Garbage Out*: Stay in tune with your thoughts. When negative thoughts enter your mind, visually picture a garbage can in front

of you, and toss the negative thoughts and self-talk into the trash can. Remember much of how we see a situation or respond is controlled by how we feel and think about what is going on around us. Take charge and control your reactions through your thoughts.

CHAPTER 4 SUMMARY

School administrators by the virtue of their positions and roles in schools are subject to encounter criticism, stress, and anxiety. Dealing with criticism, negativity, stress, and anxiety does impact the emotional, social, and physical well-being of individuals over time. Principals need to know how to manage and handle the negative side effects of unpopular decisions and actions. They must remain focused on the goals of the school and continue to do what is best for the organization regardless of whether they have the total support of their school staff.

This chapter briefly discussed techniques, strategies, and suggested interventions currently used by school administrators to manage and cope with criticism, negativity, stress, and anxiety. School leaders have been able to protect and support themselves by implementing supplemental resources and personal strategies to maintain their effectiveness. It is important that school administrators use school-level resources and other strategies to remain positive and centered.

GOING DEEPER

Time to Reflect

1. How do you cope with or handle criticism, stress, negativity, and anxiety?
2. Have you received negative criticism or feedback that helped you? If yes, briefly explain how you were helped.
3. How do you receive negative criticism or feedback from colleagues and associates?
4. What strategies or techniques do you use to address negative encounters?
5. Are you currently experiencing early signs of stress? If so, how do you plan to address them?
6. Develop a plan with a specific time frame to relieve stress and anxiety on the job.
7. Are there any strategies or techniques that are more effective for you than others? If so, why?
8. List strategies or tips you are interested in implementing to try.

9. Are there any strategies you would recommend to a colleague or associate that are not included in this chapter?
10. Seek input from former colleagues and associates. How do they manage stress?
11. Develop a calendar of activities to implement for a month.
12. Select a trusted friend or mentor to serve as your accountability partner. Ask for feedback after a predetermined time frame. If you had positive changes, what do you think contributed to those changes?
13. Write five positive affirmations for yourself. How will the affirmations help you in remaining positive and creative throughout the day?

Chapter Five

If Only You Could Do It Over Again

Looking Back and Moving Forward

> *Life can only be understood backwards; but it must be lived forwards.*—Søren Kierkegaard

School leaders often spend years performing their job without taking time to look back on what they've accomplished. They don't think about which decisions or strategies worked or didn't work. School leaders don't seek pats on the back, positive comments, trophies, or high accolades. Why not? Wouldn't taking time to sit, think, and reflect help school administrators improve and grow? Most people advise individuals not to look back but keep moving and forging ahead. Just strive to do better daily and let whatever happened yesterday stay there. Look toward tomorrow, not yesterday.

Every year thousands of individuals are ending long and rewarding careers as school administrators. They feel good about their past accomplishments and are looking forward to starting new careers, retirement, travel, and spending time with families or friends. Some administrators continue to serve in part-time capacities with their current employing school system or serve their communities in other meaningful ways. That final year of tenure as principal is usually focused on completing special projects, making sure all end-of-the-year tasks are finished, and preparing the way for their successor. Time is not spent on reflecting.

Research emphasizes the impact the simple act of reflecting has on professional growth and development for teachers and schools. Do school leaders use reflection to improve their overall effectiveness as instructional leaders and change agents? Also, if selected former school administrators reflect on their past performance, would they behave differently? Would they have the same leadership style and focus? Do they have any second thoughts regarding their leadership? Are there strategies or techniques they would recommend to current colleagues, aspiring leaders, and their successors?

Chapter 5 examines self-reflection and self-reflecting as tools to help principals improve their overall effectiveness. School administrators are encouraged to examine themselves professionally and personally to determine areas or skills to further develop or enhance. Strategies are presented to serve as guidelines for implementing and scheduling reflection as a component of the workday. Additionally, selected retired former elementary principals share their thoughts as part of a reflection exercise for this book. Their responses are enlightening and food for thought for current and aspiring school leaders.

REFLECTION

Why do we need to look back? What role does reflection play in our growth? Do school leaders gain anything from looking back on past performances, previous actions, or past mistakes? Are there any benefits from taking time to reflect? Do school leaders use self-reflecting as a tool to find more efficient and effective ways to improve their leadership skills? Results of an informal survey of selected elementary principals indicated that reflecting during the workday was minimal or not done at all. Most of the principals were focused on surviving and handling crises that arose to the best of their ability and knowledge.

There are benefits to reflecting and taking time to think about past actions, decisions, and encounters. By reflecting on their past experiences, principals can think more clearly about the experience and lesson learned from the situation. This process enables them to gain a clearer understanding of the situation and decide what they might do differently if the situation occurs again. Administrators who reflect on their experiences regularly allow for effective and continuous growth. Additionally, school administrators who incorporate reflection as part of their workday serve as excellent models for teachers and students. Reflection determines next steps.

The Benefits and Value of Reflection

Everyone benefits from reflection. Reflection enables principals to process, understand, and make meaning of their work and life experiences—good and bad. School leaders also promote and encourage growth for themselves and others by promoting the use of reflection as a regular routine. Reflection enables school administrators to make the most of their job experience regardless of the school setting. The purpose of reflection is not to dwell on negative things, but to encourage school leaders to examine negative experiences positively and obtain new or different perspectives. Reflecting on successes and failures allows school leaders to transfer new insights gained to other similar situations.

Strengthen Leadership through Self-Reflection

School leaders need to spend time examining themselves as well as their experiences and job performance. Self-reflection offers school administrators the opportunity to self-assess strengths and weaknesses to improve their effectiveness and increase productivity. Principals spend an enormous amount of time running from situation to situation putting out fires and responding to the needs of school clientele. They need to remove themselves from the busy noise of the day to reflect on their beliefs, skills, and personal and professional goals. If reflection is a powerful tool for school leaders, why are some leaders not using reflection to grow?

Reflection gives school administrators the opportunity to pause during their chaotic day and sort through observations, experiences, and incidents.

By taking time to self-reflect, principals can look inward to acquire a better understanding of their strengths, weaknesses, drives, values, and emotions. This activity empowers them to improve their skills as instructional leaders and strengthen their emotional stability. School administrators should ask themselves questions periodically to monitor their progress and growth. Do they know their strengths and areas needing improvement? Which areas are priorities for improvement? Do they have the proper resources available when needed? What is their plan of action? Do they understand what is important and where their focus should be?

End-of-the-year reflection questions such as *What made this school year good or bad? Did we achieve everything we set out to? What surprised us— good or bad? What did we do well? What did we learn?* and *Where did we falter?* activate thoughts. Reflecting and responding to the questions foster and encourage administrators' professional growth and effectiveness as they gain additional insight and understanding from their experiences. The benefits of reflection or self-reflecting assist principals in:

- *Letting go:* Take a step back from an unpleasant experience and take a deep breath. Reflecting on the situation after obtaining calmness enables leaders to think decisively about the incident and move in a different direction. Additionally, letting go is another way to cope with sorrow and disappointment, as well as knowing what to be grateful for in a certain situation.
- *Gaining clarity:* Write down what you learned and what the next step should be if the incident or encounter occurs again.

- *Making decisions:* Decide what to do next after letting go of situations and obtaining clarity. The decision(s) should be in line with your school and professional goal(s).

Effective Reflection Practices

Reflection will not become a part of school leaders' days without a plan of action. To take advantage of this valuable tool for growth and professional development, instructional leaders need to remove themselves from the business and noise of the day to reflect. Effective practices school leaders can implement to foster and encourage reflection are setting aside a time to reflect, establishing an accountability partner, monitoring progress visually, writing thoughts in a journal, and sharing or discussing what is learned with others. Although reflection does not come naturally to everyone, it can be acquired and become a habit for school leaders.

Listed below are suggested questions school administrators may ask themselves to help guide thoughts as they reflect on each day's events or encounters:

- What happened?
- Who were the main people involved?
- What went well?
- What could I have done better?
- What role did the main people play in the situation?
- What was I thinking when the incident or situation occurred?
- How did I feel about the incident or situation?
- What was my position?
- Was my experience good or bad?
- What sense did I make of the situation or incident?
- Have I had any similar situations or incidents?
- How did I handle incidents or situations in the past?
- Did I gain any insights or different perspectives about the situation or incident?
- Did I accomplish what I planned?
- Is there anything else I could have done?
- What would I do differently, if a similar incident or situation occurs?
- What lesson or lessons did I learn from the incident or situation?
- What were the outcomes?
- Do I have the appropriate skills, knowledge, or resources needed to assist in the future?
- What insight(s) have I gained from the incident or situation?

It is evident school administrators can maximize their potential and leadership skills by taking the opportunity to reflect on their experiences. To take advantage of reflecting as a process, leaders must schedule a specific time to reflect. Lessons acquired from looking back on past experiences will assist them in handling future situations and incidents more effectively. Self-reflecting on strengths and weaknesses tied to specific leadership skills and techniques equips principals with the ability to grow and develop continuously as school managers and change agents.

LOOKING BACK TO MOVE FORWARD

How many of us have walked down memory lane and thought about what we would change or do differently, if another opportunity was presented? We know taking the time to reflect and grow from lessons learned helps administrators provide professional growth for themselves, teachers, and students. Are there any benefits from looking back after completing a career? Chapter 5 explores this question with selected former principals. Current and aspiring administrators will gain tips from former principals who candidly share thoughts about their past experiences and lessons learned.

If given the opportunity to revisit and reflect on their tenure as elementary principals, would they behave differently based on past experiences and lessons learned? Would they have a different focus or goal? A selected group of principals was asked to reflect on their past experiences as school-level administrators. A small sample of retired former school leaders was asked to reflect and respond to a series of questions about their school leadership experiences. Six former school leaders are retired and one former principal is currently employed. The school leaders were employed in Camden County School System located in Kingsland, Georgia.

The selected former and current school leaders worked at the elementary, middle, and high school levels. They began their careers as classroom teachers. It is important for the reader to note that although the sample is small, their responses are applicable to other school leaders in the country. The ideas and feelings expressed are food for thought for current and aspiring administrators.

School Leader A

What was the most pleasant aspect or part of your job?

The highlight of a thirty-four-year career, seventeen years in the classroom and seventeen years as an administrator, was connecting with children and their families. Seeing students excel in many areas and overcoming barriers to their learning as a teacher and leader was more important than anything else.

What was the most difficult aspect or part of your job?

Being one of the special education sites for the county and dealing with the different exceptionalities and serving them in the regular education setting was very challenging. Principals often must resolve service issues or situations encountered even when they don't have the most appropriate care setting and best trained teachers possible. This caused internal struggles because of the lack of satisfaction with the quality and amount of care provided for special-needs students and their families. Decisions made regarding their care and the least-restricted environment also created difficulty.

What would you do differently if you had another opportunity?

More time would be spent researching educational methods and grants to enrich the lives of the students and teachers. During graduate school, studying about the Key School Project piqued an interest in learning how they focused on all modalities and how students learned best. A greater effort would be made to explore more innovative methods and programs for the teacher teams.

Where would your focus be?

To alleviate the problem of nonreaders leaving the elementary school, the focus would be on finding the best programs to teach reading. Why is it we have highly trained staff and still have students leaving us as nonreaders? This should be top priority. Children who can read accomplish whatever they put their mind to. Being readers equips children to meet challenges and obtain knowledge through reading.

What type of leader would you be because of your prior experience or lessons learned?

More organized and a better manager of time. Adequate time spent on research would enable the implementation of effective intervention programs for regular education and special-needs students.

What type(s) of school leaders do students, teachers, and parents need?

School leaders who are devoted to developing and building relationships to serve as effective advocates are needed. Families must trust their school administrator and know that they are willing to listen and provide the best educational care for all types of students.

Do you have advice or recommendations for current and aspiring school leaders?

School leaders need an assigned mentor or should participate in a shadowing program for two years to assist them in learning how to become an effective instructional leader. School leaders need a sounding board and the opportunity to collaborate with others for successful leadership.

What training(s) or experience(s) should universities and colleges add to prepare new school leaders?

Mentoring and shadowing programs should be a component of college or university educational leadership programs. Also, school systems need to allot time for mentors and mentees to collaborate and discuss events.

Given a second chance, would you still aspire to be a school leader?

Absolutely! Being called by God to teach and lead fulfilled my life and provided challenging, exciting, and rewarding days everyday as an educator and leader.

School Leader B

What was the most pleasant aspect or part of your job?

The joy of teaching transferred easily from a classroom teacher role to the school leader role. Teachers, paraprofessionals, bus drivers, substitute teachers, and college students benefited from this joy through the years. Nothing was more enjoyable than seeing the successful implementation of an effective strategy, classroom instructional practice, technique, or skill. Effective instruction results in student achievement.

What was the most difficult aspect or part of your job?

Constant change. Elections brought new leaders into the position of power and authority. Everyone had different ideas on how to fix public education. Not all changes are bad. Any change, however, does require time for implementation. Time is also needed for understanding, training, application, and evaluation of its effectiveness. Educators rarely have the luxury of the time needed. In a few short years, there is another election and the cycle repeats itself. Feeling like a puppet on a string, as the school leader, there was no voice or authority to make any changes for the good of the school. Staff were encouraged to adapt to changes and implement what was required by the state and/or school system.

What would you do differently, if you had another opportunity?

Delegate more and prioritize what needed to be accomplished based on school goals and objectives. Much time was spent doing tasks that others could have easily performed. For example, planning Field Day and making it happen does not require a school leader's attention. Physical education teachers have the knowledge and experience to plan a Field Day event for the school. Sharing and giving responsibilities to others not only frees time for a school leader to handle more significant matters, but also builds trust and confidence in the relationship between the leader and the staff.

Where would your focus be?

Effective classroom instruction is a top priority. Spending time supporting teachers in classrooms would continue to be a focus.

What type of school leader would you be because of your prior experience or lessons learned?

Preferably an instructional leader. There would be a concerted effort to find more ways to recognize and celebrate staff, highlighting instruction and achievement.

What type(s) of school leaders do students, teachers, and parents need?

Students need the opportunity to learn in a nurturing and safe environment. Teachers need to be able to assess students' needs and plan instruction that'll enable students to achieve. They also need support and encouragement from school administrators and supervisors. They all need someone who:

- listens and respects them as people;
- calls them by name;
- cares;
- admits when they are wrong;
- forgives;

- learns;
- shows enthusiasm;
- keeps an open door; and
- asks for and values input.

What help or assistance would you offer current and aspiring leaders?

Be confident in the ability to make decisions. Seek guidance from those who are older and wiser. Never forget that you have been entrusted with the responsibility and noble task of leading a group of individuals into the future. Strive to find the strengths, skills, and gifts in each person and develop them to the best of your ability. Recognize, accept, and celebrate differences.

What training(s) or experience(s) should universities and colleges add to prepare new school leaders?

Internships with successful, experienced school leaders should be offered as a part of their educational leadership programs. They also should seek current leaders to present in classes as a resource to answer questions and talk about the day-to-day operations of managing schools.

Given a second chance, would you still aspire to be a school leader?

Yes! Although working in the educational arena has become more challenging, it's still appealing and desirable. Associating with children, families, teachers, and the community was very enjoyable. Everyone deserves the opportunity to be educated.

School Leader C

What was the most pleasant aspect or part of your job?

The daily contact with students. Because of the love for working with young children, becoming a teacher was a number one priority. Young children are excited learning about new things. They are a captive audience if you keep their interest and meet their learning needs.

What was the most difficult aspect or part of your job?

The most difficult part was dealing with some of the personnel issues. Another difficult part was keeping up with never-ending paperwork and additional responsibilities initiated at the system level. Always being held responsible for teachers' inappropriate comments and actions was challenging.

What would you do differently, if you had another opportunity?

More time would be spent on developing and building relationships with students and teachers. Also, more time would be spent communicating beliefs and expectations to faculty, staff, students, and parents.

What would your focus be?

The focus would be on fostering and developing resiliency in students. Teachers would receive training on what can be done in classrooms to foster and encourage resiliency.

What type of school leader would you be because of prior experiences or lessons learned?

A stronger change agent and relationship builder. Students and families have a greater need for social services than ever before. Many families are stressed and in need of social/mental health services. In some cases, students and their families need advocates to help them navigate the social services system. There is a need to have a leader who will have time to communicate with students and their families.

What type of school leaders do students, teachers, and parents need?

They need school leaders who have a genuine and sincere heart for children and their families. They also need a leader who is empathetic and not sympathetic. Parents and students need school leaders who are knowledgeable advocates.

What help or assistance would you offer current and aspiring school leaders?

Offer to be a sounding board, resource, and mentor. Be confident and be true to your values. Don't let criticism or negative comments reduce you as a person. Accept the fact that you will not make everyone happy, and always do what is good and right for children.

What should universities and colleges add to prepare and train new school leaders?

Try to provide more real-to-life experiences in class through videos, demonstrations, and site visits. Partner with local schools and arrange panel discussions with current school-level administrators. Have students shadow experienced school leaders for several days.

Given a second chance, would you still aspire to be a school leader?

Yes, but for a shorter period. School or family counseling would have been pursued as an additional career.

School Leader D

What was the most pleasant aspect or part of your job?

The most enjoyable aspect of being a school leader was the act of leading. An experienced, dedicated, and caring staff is not hard to lead. Although there are always demanding situations to manage, having the courage and strength to make tough decisions was rewarding. Second to enjoying the leadership role was building lasting relationships with teachers, students, and their families. One enjoyable annual event was rewarding students with books through a special reading club honoring a deceased former school administrator.

What was the most difficult aspect or part of your job?

The most difficult aspect of the job as school leader was assuming the position with new or relatively new personnel in three key positions: assistant principal, office manager, and guidance counselor. Learning the culture and nuances of the business of school may have been much easier had personnel been more experienced at the school. In reflection, however, this situation did present opportunities to cultivate relationships without preconceived ideas or notions.

What would you do differently, if you had another opportunity?

The importance of understanding and appreciating parent involvement became more and more apparent over the years. Parents are often only called when there is a crisis or behavior-related issue. Of course, time is a factor, but there would be a commitment to making daily positive phone calls to parents.

What would your focus be?

Spending more time in classrooms and meaningful daily visits would be beneficial. Focusing on teaching and learning, particularly through conversations with teachers and students, would be very helpful and beneficial.

What type of leader would you be because of past experiences or lessons learned?

One thing that would not change, given the opportunity, would be ministering in a servant leadership role. Meeting the needs of teachers and staff who directly affect the outcomes of students is critical.

What type of administrator do students, teachers, and parents really need?

Servant leadership is what school communities need. No one has all the answers, but attempting to meet needs by being available and answering calls, whether spoken or unspoken, creates a culture of trust among those who need and deserve it.

What do students, teachers, and parents really need?

Having learned so much more than curriculum since leaving the school leadership role, it's imperative that learning should include aspects of social and emotional well-being. School personnel need professional learning in this area, students need support during the day, and parents need constant and consistent information about social and emotional well-being.

What help or assistance would you offer current or aspiring school leaders?

Focus should be on curriculum and social/emotional learning, while cultivating trusting relationships with those within the school community. Paperwork, managing a building, and other minutiae can detract from the most critical aspects of school. A daily reminder is needed to reconnect with what's important.

What should universities and colleges add to prepare and train new school leaders?

There are some aspects of learning about school leadership that are on-the-job training. Universities and colleges can only minimally prepare leaders. School leaders need a course on understanding and managing more severe behaviors and other traits. More and more students are entering school without emotional regulation. School leaders need to know the functions of behavior and how best to manage their responses to them.

Given a second chance, would you still aspire to be a school leader?

Yes! Other than teaching, being a school leader was more enjoyable than any other job or role held. Teachers and students need cheerleaders and supporters. It was an honor to attempt to fill those roles.

School Leader E

What was the most pleasant aspect or part of your job?

The most important aspect was working with students who had social, emotional, behavioral, or academic challenges and seeing them flourish.

What was the most difficult aspect or part of your job?

The most challenging aspect of the job was dealing with disgruntled parents.

What would you do differently, if you had another opportunity?

Be more patient working with others.

What would your focus be?

Now there is more focus on academics. Therefore, there would be more focus on academics.

What type of school leader would you be based on past experiences and lessons learned?

Be more diplomatic in some areas and autocratic in some.

What type of administrator do students, teachers, and parents really need?

One who is compassionate, patient, kindhearted, knowledgeable, willing to learn, and student focused.

What do students, teachers, and parents really need?

The same as the above.

What help or assistance would you offer current and aspiring school leaders?

Know your families, know your students, be patient and flexible, and focus on academics. You will make mistakes and make many of them; just learn from them!

What should universities and colleges add to prepare and train new leaders?

Teach how to make the best of their planning time and collaboration time.

Given a second chance, would you still aspire to be a school leader?

Yes, if younger. Too old to learn new tricks and deal with the political tenor of administration.

School Leader F

What was the most pleasant aspect or part of your job?

The most rewarding aspect was encouraging and watching the evolution of teachers becoming leaders in the school. School leaders should not so much be an instructional leader as a leader of instructors. Thoroughly enjoyed empowering teachers who have outstanding work ethics, are good communicators, and get superior results. When teachers know they have earned their principal's confidence, they become the expert in the school, and in many cases the district, in their subject and grade. They are self-motivated and in turn motivate other teachers around them to perform at a higher level.

What was the most difficult aspect or part of the job for you?

Maintaining good student discipline is the most difficult part of the job. This must be established before quality instruction can occur. Although this is extremely time consuming, it is imperative that students are respectful and follow school rules. Handling discipline incidents and giving consequences in a fair and thorough manner is very difficult and can take a lot out of an administrator. No matter how much experience a school leader has with curriculum, if they cannot establish a school with good discipline, they will be ineffective.

What would you do differently, if you had another opportunity?

Do a better job interviewing and hiring teachers. Also, be quicker to non-renew teachers in their first year if experiencing difficulties. This is one area in which individuals would not be given the benefit of the doubt again.

What would your focus be?

Publicly praising and acknowledging those who are doing an excellent job.

What type of school leader would you be based on past experiences and lessons learned?

Continue to be firm, fair, and consistent. Wouldn't be hesitant to point out areas staff need to improve. A greater effort would be made to praise those who are doing an excellent job.

What type of administrator do students, teachers, and parents really need?

They need someone who is polite, friendly, matter of fact, and honest.

What do students, teachers, and parents really need?

See the above.

What help or assistance would you offer current and aspiring school leaders?

Be very grounded in all aspects of the running of the school. This includes student discipline, transportation issues, maintenance, custodial, school law, and curriculum.

What should universities and colleges add to prepare and train new school leaders?

Focus should be on areas mentioned in the previous question. School leaders should have at least one year's experience (internship) doing nothing but handling discipline and school operational issues.

Given a second chance, would you still aspire to be a school leader?

School leadership does change your personality and takes a toll, but it is very rewarding in the end. So, yes.

The selected former school leaders willingly participated in the reflecting activity by stepping back and thinking about their past experiences, challenges, and lessons learned. Although they were employed in the same school system and served during separate times as school leaders, there are several areas of commonality among them. Each school leader became an educator because of their interest and love for learning. They became teachers to influence and nurture others. Passing on a legacy, a love, and passion for life-long learning is a rewarding commitment.

Another common characteristic is their desire to help and serve others. Each school leader expressed serving teachers, students, and families by connecting students and families with appropriate emotional and social resources. This need is becoming more critical as families too face ever-changing challenges and stressors. To serve students and families effectively, principals must think out of the box or seek other avenues to meet the needs of students and their families. School leaders will need to venture outside the confines of their building to link their school with supplemental resources and services not offered by their school or system.

Additionally, the selected former principals who were surveyed recommended that universities and colleges add an internship or mentoring component to their programs to train or prepare leaders. This shows the need to reexamine what schools of higher education are providing for aspiring school leaders. Most of the former principals seemed to be advocating for more on-the-job experience for future school administrators. Perhaps as we continue to experience the effects of federal and state mandates, budget cuts, curriculum updates, and changes, authentic trainings will increase the production of more effective school leaders.

Finally, love for their profession as school leaders is evidenced throughout their responses. They seemed to remain focused and committed to their clientele despite challenges and changes. Each former principal surveyed viewed school leadership as a very rewarding endeavor. No one expressed regrets about devoting themselves to students, teachers, and families as a career. This selected group of school leaders seemed to possess principles and qualities that helped them stay the course. Their past experiences and lessons learned serve as a viable resource for current and aspiring school administrators.

LOOKING BACK WRAP-UP

Given the opportunity to reflect on past experiences and lessons learned, selected former administrators were able to objectively identify challenges and share areas they would focus on if presented another chance to lead a school. It is evident that the former principals' responses were shaped by their individual experiences and lessons learned. Each person had challenging areas and pleasant aspects as principals during their tenure. Some of the challenges noted were meeting needs of special education students and providing appropriate services, handling discipline, and dealing with parent issues. The importance of improving instruction was emphasized by all.

CHAPTER 5 SUMMARY

The life of a school leader is full of challenges and unexpected events. In this chapter, the author examines the role reflection and self-reflection play to provide continuous professional and personal growth for school administrators. Setting aside time to think about situations and examine lessons learned enables school leaders to gain different perspectives and insight into how to handle situations or incidents more effectively. Also, a selected group of former school leaders shared their reflection responses on past experiences and lessons learned during their tenure as principals.

GOING DEEPER

Time to Reflect

1. Do you see reflection or self-reflection as viable tools to implement as a part of your daily schedule?
2. How are you planning to implement reflection during your workday?
3. Generate a list of questions to jump-start your thinking.
4. Do you use reflection with teachers?
5. When is the best time for you to set aside to reflect or self-reflect during the school day?
6. Select someone to be your accountability partner for your reflecting or self-reflection journey.
7. Develop a monthly reflection plan. Share the plan with a colleague or mentor.
8. What areas or skills do you need to improve or strengthen based on your reflection or self-reflection activity?
9. Jot down lessons learned from recent circumstances and situations.
10. Brainstorm strategies to model reflection for your teachers.
11. Briefly review the challenges expressed by the former school leaders. Are you experiencing any of their challenges?
12. If you responded "yes" to the above question, brainstorm strategies to help you address the challenge(s).
13. What aspect of your job is pleasant for you? Briefly explain why.

14. Schedule a set time to meet with a mentor, colleague, or close associate to exchange ideas and tips about school leadership.
15. Informally survey retired former school leaders in your area. Compare their responses to the selected leaders' responses surveyed in this book. Are there any similarities?
16. Arrange to visit a school leader in a school system close to you. Note tips, ideas, or strategies to consider implementing in your building.

Conclusion

This has been a delightful and rewarding journey. Being a school leader has been a very fascinating and interesting position as an educator. School leaders who balance their personal and professional lives operate effective schools that produce lifelong learners and successful citizens. Administrators must nurture themselves and approach each day with patience and a positive attitude. There are no perfect teachers, students, parents, or school administrators. Base all decisions on core values, beliefs, and principles held. Stay focused and purposeful. Keep loving children, teachers, and families. If you do so, you'll be able to stay the course.

Special thanks are extended to the former and current school leaders who willingly responded to the reflection survey questions featured in this book. They have served as excellent role models and mentors during my career.

Bibliography

Bassett, Lucinda. *From Panic to Power: Proven Techniques to Calm Your Anxieties, Conquer Your Fears, and Put You in Control of Your Life*. New York: HarperCollins, 1995.
Boyadjian, Lucie, David Christensen, Larry Davis, Tamara Fahmi, Michelle Gayle, Brian Hazeltine, Brenda Hedden, Bonita Henderson, et al. "Principals Offer 30 Ways to Fight Stress." *Education World*, April 2015. www.educationworld.com/a_admin/admin/admin394.shtml.
Branson, Robert. *Coping with Difficult People*. New York: Anchor Press Doubleday, 1981.
Burrell, Brian. *The Words We Live By*. New York: Free Press, 1997.
Danielson, Lana. "Fostering Reflection." *Educational Leadership*, February 2009. www.ascd.org/publications/educational-leadership/feb09/num05-reflection.aspx.
Ellis, Albert. *How to Control Your Anxiety Before It Controls You*. New York: The Citadel Press, 1998.
Ersozlu, Alpay. "School Principals' Reflective Leadership Skills through the Eyes of Science and Math Teachers." *International Journal of Environmental Science Education* 11, no. 5 (2016): 801–8.
Howe, Randy. *The Quotable Teacher*. Guilford, CT: Lyons Press, 2003.
Kovary, Giselle. "The Value of Self Reflection." *NGen*, December 2015. www.ngenperformance.com/blog/leadership-2/the-value-of-self-reflection.
Kraemer, Harry. "How Self-Reflection Can Make You a Better Leader." *Kellogg Insight*, December 2016. https://insight.kellogg.northwestern.edu/article/how-self-reflection-can-make-you-a-better-leader.
LaRoche, Loreta. *Relax—You May Only Have a Few Minutes Left. Using the Power of Humor to Overcome Stress in Your Life and Work*. New York: Random House, 1998.
Mendels, Pamela. "The Effective Principal." *Learning Forward* 33, no. 1 (2012): 54–58.
Penick, Dana. "Reflection: An Essential Habit for Professional Development." *The Leader in Me Symposium*, January 2015. www.theleaderinmeblog.org/reflection-an-essential-habit-for-professional-development.
Porter, Jennifer. "Why You Should Make Time for Self-Reflection (Even If You Hate Doing It)." *Harvard Business Review*, March 2017. https://hbr.org/2017/03/why-you-should-make-time-for-self-reflection-even-if-you-hate-doing-it.
Quinn, Tracy. *Quotable Women of the Twentieth Century*. New York: W. Morrow, 1999.
Riley, Jo. "How Can Senior Leaders Improve Their Reflective Practice?" *The Guardian*, March 2013. www.theguardian.com/teacher-network-blog/2013/mar07/school-leaders-strategic-reflective-thinking-teaching-schedule.
Shanahan, John. *The Most Brilliant Thoughts of All Times in Two Lines or Less*. New York: Cliff Street Books, 1999.

Sternberg, Ruth. "The Ultimate Stress." *American Association of School Superintendents*, September 2001. www.aasa.org/SchoolAdministratorArticle.aspx?id=10740.

Yocco, Victor. "Dwelling on the Past: The Importance of Self-Reflection (Part 2)." *Smashing Magazine*, September 5, 2017. www.smashingmagazine.com/2017/09/importance-project-retrospectives-part-1.

Zilvold, Freek. "Benefits of Self-Reflection." *Zilvold Coaching and Training*, October 2016. www.zilvold.com/benefits-of-self-reflection.

About the Author

Sheila E. Sapp has devoted forty-four years to education, learning, children, and families. She has served as a classroom teacher, assistant principal, curriculum director, and principal during her career as an educator. Sheila recently retired from the Camden County Schools System as principal of Crooked River Elementary School, located in St. Marys, Georgia. Her school was recognized as a 2002 School of Excellence and a Title I Rewards for High Academic Achievement School for five consecutive years (2012–2016). Dr. Sapp will be working in the fall as a part-time instructor for the College of Coastal Georgia in Brunswick, Georgia. Also, she is cofounder of Sapp and Bruce Educational Consulting, LLC.

Sapp is a graduate of the University of Georgia with an education doctorate degree in supervision and curriculum. She also holds a master's in reading education (K–12) from Glassboro State College (now Rowan University) in Glassboro, New Jersey, and an educational specialist degree in administration from Georgia Southern University, Statesboro, Georgia. Sheila has authored two books, *The Learning House* and *Best Practices for New School Administrators*. Additionally, Sapp has conducted workshops for teachers and parents on conferencing and motivating students. She resides in Woodbine, Georgia, with her husband, Everette.

www.ingramcontent.com/pod-product-compliance
Lightning Source LLC
Chambersburg PA
CBHW032029230426
43671CB00005B/246